GET OFF YOUR ASS AND INVEST

A Tale of Two Brothers and a Mutual Fund

ZACK DOROBIALA

ISBN–13: 978-1-945431-24-1

Printed in the United States of America.

Dedicated to my brother, Adam

Special thanks to my good friend Mattie and my godfather, Bobby

Contents

Chapter 1
Introduction

I've spent years lecturing Adam, my brother, about money. I have shown him every chart, table, and graph in existence about investing, and he has not seemed to listen. Unlike me, Adam is right-brained. He is more creative, intuitive, and emotionally invested in decisions. Left-brained people like me want to see the numbers and data, but my brother needs a little more convincing.

Is one school of thought better than the other? Not necessarily. Because we are wired differently, different arguments appeal to us. So, in a last-ditch effort to get my brother to take my advice on money, I have sat down at my computer and written arguments that will appeal to both of us.

I want my brother (and you) to become a better and more educated financial investor. To do that, my points must be diverse and appeal to various people with a variety of thinking styles. I believe that you are a few short principles away from being a more diverse investor.

That sounds like a sales pitch, but I honestly think this book outlines concepts that can help you manage your money better. The goal is for these concepts to be accessible for the left brained, the right-brained, the high-school dropouts, the PhDs, and everyone in between. You can become a wealthier person by learning more about money, and I am here to tell you how.

Index funds. That's the answer to the question I'm sure you're asking: "How are you going to make me money? What's this magical money secret you have?" Index funds, or passively managed funds, are a group of stocks seeking to represent a larger market. If that doesn't make sense to you yet, that's OK. I'll explain that more later.

Before we begin, no, I am not going to take 2% of your portfolio. No, I am not going to sell you on the next hot stock. No, I do not work for some investment firm or insurance company.

Ten years ago, I had no idea how the stock market worked. I was even more clueless as to how to act on what little knowledge I did have. Lucky for me, I was recommended a plethora of books on investing. I got a degree from Niagara University in mathematics, actuarial science, and philosophy. I then used that degree to become a behavioral economist. I read countless dry investing books, suffered through too many textbooks, and took everything from fundamentals of investing to math of finance. All so I could tell you in the simplest of terms what kinds of techniques you can implement to become a wealthier long-term investor. I am going to show you why investing in index funds will not only save you time and heartache but also save you lots and lots of "one percent fees," which magically or mathematically can add up to thousands of dollars.

Before I launch into my brother's story, his money, and me, I want to quickly explain one tool developed by William Marston in 1928 that compared left-brained and right-brained thinking styles. This model is called DiSC,[1] and it breaks those styles down into four categories: dominance, influence, steadiness, and conscientiousness. There are two categories of left-brained people and two categories of right-brained people.

If someone leans toward the dominance (D) side of the spectrum, they are likely more leadership-orientated, blunt, straightforward, and confident. Those who thrive off others' energy, like to work within groups, and are very optimistic sit on the influence (I) side of

1 Marston, W. M., & Parkes, F. (1928). *Emotions of normal people*. Routledge.

the method. If someone is calm, emotional, and caring about others' feelings and emotions, they fit most closely with the steadiness (S) category of thinkers. If numbers, logical reasoning, and accuracy motivate someone, they lean towards the conscientiousness (C) category.

This test does not place you strictly into one category of the DiSC method; instead, it gives you percentages of which directions you lean. This is helpful because you obviously aren't precisely right- or left-brained in everything you do. Different situations bring out other characteristics, thinking styles, and learning patterns in all of us. We are all unique and learn in our own particular way.

Sometimes, you think you may be making the most precise and concise argument, and the person across from you is just not getting it. For example, I am more left-brained and lean heavily towards the C side of the DiSC method. Therefore, I like to make all my decisions with statistics, charts, and logic. These are all great tools if I am trying to convince or be convinced by another left-brained person. However, when I try to teach my brother how to better manage his money, those things just do not click for him, and that's OK. Adam prefers to use emotion and creativity to draw conclusions. To make this book accessible to a broader audience. I have attempted to write this book so that it speaks to every side of the DiSC spectrum. If you are interested in your thinking style, you can learn more about it at discprofile.com.

A popular saying goes, "Everybody is a genius. But if you judge a fish by its ability to climb a tree, it will live its whole life believing that it is stupid."

This well-known illustration shows that not everyone learns or completes tasks in the same way. While climbing a tree might be a piece of cake for a monkey, a salmon will come up short every time. Vice versa, a monkey cannot swim up a waterfall as a salmon can. There is nothing inherently better about either animal; they are merely different. Being right- or left-brained is similar: It may be a lot harder for a right-brained person to comprehend charts and graphs, and it can be harder to convince a left-brained person using emotion and feelings. The point is that every thinking style has its strengths and weaknesses and should not be judged on the same task or informational absorption.

With all that being said, when teaching you about index funds, I want to try to appeal to all different kinds of learners and thinkers—visual, logical, blunt, and emotional. I want to make you a better investor and a wealthier person regardless of how you think.

Along with teaching different learners, I want to stress that no one is too young or too poor to start investing today. I will discuss in chapters 3 and 4 why compounding and $1 fund minimums make the last statement true.

Let us now dive into the story where it all started: lunch with Bobby.

Chapter 2

Lunch with Bobby

Core Principle:
**Leave the percent talk to the statisticians.
Let us talk about money.**

In 2015, I was an undergraduate at Niagara University. I wanted to know more about money, investing, and planning my financial future. So, I asked my godfather, Bobby, to lunch to teach me everything he knew. We sat down over some excellent sushi; being in Buffalo, NY, they even had a beef on weck sushi (I was not a fan, but Bobby loved it), and I listened to his advice and absorbed his financial wisdom for three hours.

Bobby taught me so much that day, but one of the most valuable topics I learned was index funds. He described it as a fund that seeks to match the performance of the stocks within the index. Bobby provided me with an example and explored in detail the S&P 500 index: a share of that index invests you in all 500 companies within the index, allowing for broad diversification. The point of an index is to duplicate the returns of the stocks in the index to ultimately try to mimic the stock market.

The sushi was great—I got the spicy crab roll—and the conversation was even better. The lunch was a success, but there was one problem: Bobby was very blunt and honest with all the topics he explained. He used his D brain to teach me, a more C-brained person. Bobby is a direct person who is leadership-oriented. That is not how I learn. This discrepancy showed up even in the reading he recommended to me at the end of the conversation. He gave me an excellent book called *The Bogleheads' Guide to Investing* by Mel Lindauer, Michael LeBoeuf, and Taylor Larimore. It was an exceptional read, but I was getting so caught up in the weeds of Bobby's D argument that I sat there and did nothing for two years. You read that correctly: TWO YEARS.

Two years passed, and I picked up the book *Unshakeable* by Tony Robbins, also recommended by Bobby. Things immediately clicked for me. The book explained things in a way my C brain understood. Why would I want to mimic the stock market as a whole? Why would I want to invest in index funds? Because the stock market has historically returned 10% on average over all its years of existence. I finally saw the S&P 500 graph below, and everything finally made sense:

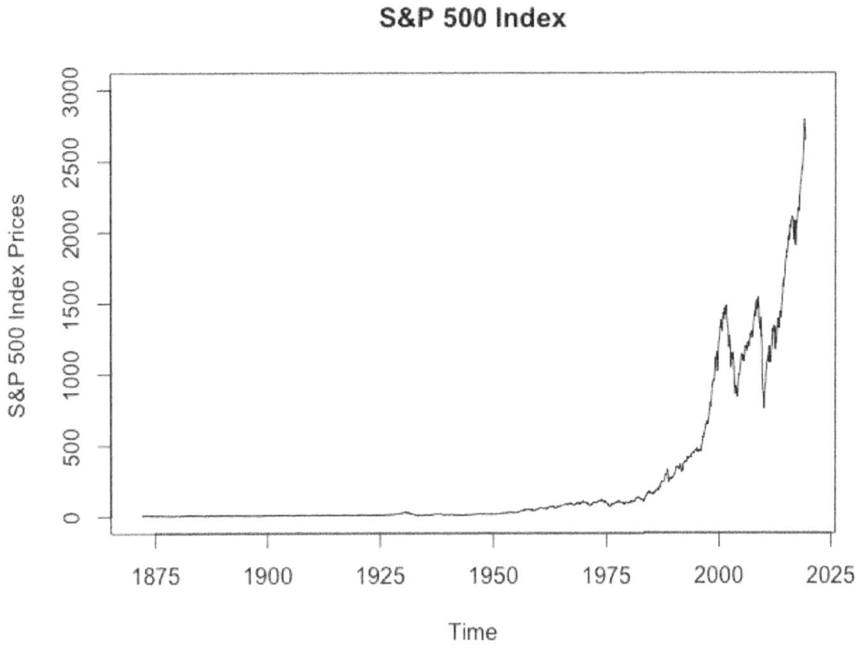

An index fund, like the S&P 500, holds a plethora of various stocks to diversify. By diversification, an investor reduces risks associated with the markets the stocks are in.

Let's say you own only Apple stock. Apple is in the tech sector. If the tech sector takes a hit for any number of reasons, the investor whose entire portfolio is in tech will take a massive hit. However, if an investor has stocks in Apple and the airline sector, an investor's overall risk is reduced. By investing in an index, you are investing in many industry sectors, all of which are moving in different directions at any given point based on sector or world events.

To put this more bluntly, for the D- and C-brained individuals, the S&P 500 index looks closely to mimic the stock market. We simulate the stock market because it has historically averaged close to 10% each year. By imitating the stock market, we can hope to average close to 10% ourselves. Guess what the S&P 500 has averaged since its inception? A little under 10%.

Using the data and starting in 1980, I created a statistical trend through the S&P 500 graph, indicated by the red line.

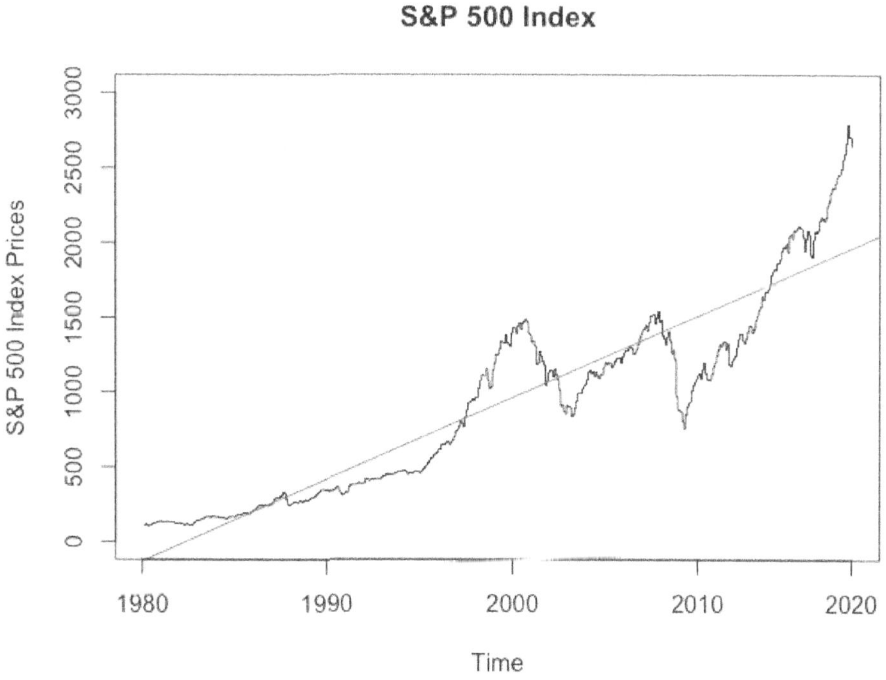

What do you notice about this graph? It trends upwards, right? When you invest in an index fund, like the S&P 500 index, you are essentially betting that the trend will continue to be upward sloping. Throughout the existence of the S&P 500, its overall trend has never been downward descending.

In the original S&P 500 graph, we notice that it is nearly flat until around 1980, so I started the chart in 1980. You must not interpret these two graphs to say that the stock market never goes down. It does (quite often), but over time, the general direction has trended upward. If it ever were to become downward sloping, that would mean the market is in for a total crash. Luckily, this has never happened before, and it would not matter what you have invested in at that point anyway.

You can see that, over 70 years, the S&P 500 has had its ups and downs. However, the average annual return over those 70 years has been around 10%. This is an incredible number for any investment. However, if you know you can pick the next Apple, stop reading this book and go do that, because that would be much more profitable. If you can get a financial advisor who claims he can beat the S&P 500 index every year and has proof of the results longer than 10 to 20 years, stop reading this book and invest with him.

The problem with picking "hot" stocks is that it is tough to do. I will not bore you with the math or terminology, but the fact of the matter is stock market returns are said to be a random walk. In terms of the stock market, a random walk means it is nearly impossible to consistently forecast what will happen in the next day, week, month, or year. Each movement is as arbitrary and sporadic as the last.

Tell me: If you could know what the stock market will do in the future, would you be content taking 2% of a portfolio for that knowledge? Of course not! It is more likely you would sell your house, car, and boat to invest everything you have. You would keep your knowledge a secret and reap the rewards of your ability to tell the future.

How do I relay this information to my brother? He does not care about graphs. He does not understand statistical trends. We both looked at these graphs but saw very different things. Adam always calls me and asks questions like "Disney is about to skyrocket; I can feel it. Any advice?" or "I hear the market is in for a downturn; should I move all my investments to gold and precious metals?" or "Tesla is the next Apple, what do you think, Zack?" or "I hear there is an oil shortage. Are we going into a recession?"

Adam already knows the big-name companies like Disney, Apple, Tesla, etc. You likely do too. The S&P 500 index is comprised of the 500 biggest companies listed on the US stock exchanges.[2] By holding a share of the S&P 500 index, you essentially own a piece of all those 500 companies. That is a good idea because the index is so diverse that it minimizes the risks associated with sector shocks—like an oil shortage. (Be careful with that last statement. It minimizes the risks, but it does not rid you of them.)

Why is it wise to diversify? Imagine if all your money was in banking before the crisis in 2008. You would have lost a lot more of your portfolio value than if you had a diversified portfolio. The point is that investing in individual stocks is active investing. To do that, you need an advisor, and she needs her cut.

I have told my brother repeatedly, "You do not know how the stock market will look any better than financial professionals will." Historically, after advisors receive their fees, investors have averaged around 5% or lower. The majority of hired professionals cannot even consistently beat the market returns.

My brother has a biology degree. He has never taken a finance course, and he only reads the news for finance information. If most people who devote their lives to understanding finance and the stock market cannot beat the market consistently, why do you think you can? That is not a knock at my brother. It sounds harsh, but that is an honest question everyone needs to ask themselves when they start thinking they can pick the next Apple.

---

2 For more information on what exact stocks comprise the S&P 500 index, visit https://www.google.com/finance/quote/.INX:INDEXSP?.

My brother is obsessed with Tesla and their cars. To help illustrate the point I am trying to make to him, I offer this illustration: Consider a hypothetical situation in which you can get the Tesla Model S, worth $75,000, and the Model 3, worth $40,000, for the same price if you wait 10 years.

Let us say an advisor yields you the average he has after fees—around 5% historically. No advisor you or I could hire has beaten the stock market index for longer than 20 years consistently. If you do not believe me, just ask your advisor for his returns each year and compare them to the S&P 500 index returns.

Adam screams out, "Zack, it's only 5%! Every time I go to the store, I am taxed at 9%!" But 5% over a 10-year window can add up to thousands of lost dollars.

Let's look at a simple example of my brother buying the lowest model Tesla versus purchasing a higher-end Tesla model: Let us say you have $5,000 to invest. In one scenario, you passively invest that $5,000 into an index fund. In the second scenario, you actively invest with an advisor. Plus, an additional $300 is invested per month for 10 years. At the end of those 10 years, the index fund will have expectedly yielded you $75,500.81! The actively managed advisor portfolio would have earned you over $20,000 less: $55,013.83.

If you want to check those numbers for yourself, put those numbers in a compound interest calculator.[3] Implementing the principles laid out in this book could make a $20,486.98 difference. Choosing not to implement them means $20,000 less for a car, your child's education, or a down payment on a house. The difference of $20,000 could be the difference between paying for all of your child's education and her being obligated to take out loans.

As you read this book, my examples will show you how the difference between index returns and advisor returns will only increase and could potentially get into the hundreds of thousands of dollars lost to fees.

---

3 *Compound interest calculator*. Compound Interest Calculator | Investor.gov. (n.d.). www.investor.gov/financial-tools-calculators/calculators/compound-interest-calculator.

	Index - 10%	Advisor - 5%
Initial amount invested	$5,000	$5,000
Amount invest each month	$300	$300
Overall amount invested after 10 years	$41,000	$41,000
Years of investing	10	10
Value of investment	$75,500.81	$55,013.83

My brother could not comprehend the difference in return percentages, but I spoke his language when I translated those percentages into dollar figures. He started to understand the power of mimicking the market and how much money can be lost by losing a percentage value here or there. He also began to understand the futility of trying to forecast the next Apple.

There is only one thing worse than losing out on $20K: being out of the market for 20 years. Inflation will erode your money by 3% each year with no return attached to that -3%. Now, the $25,000 from 20 years ago only purchases $13,594.86 worth of goods.

You might ask yourself, "Why invest in the first place?" Investing allows for monetary growth and a constant machine to enable investors to retain their purchasing power throughout the years. In most of my examples, I will not include inflation for simplicity but always be mindful that indecision is also a decision that will still cost you.[4]

Before we get on to the first topic, I want you to understand that I am not bullshitting these numbers for the sake of argument. A study by Robert Arnott found that 95% of actively managed mutual funds failed to beat the stock market's average return over 15 years. Therefore, only 5%—11 out of 203—were able to beat the S&P 500 benchmark. On top of that, this was all BEFORE taxes and capital gains.[5] Most financial advisors cannot earn you the

4 St. louis fed. FRED. (n.d.). https://fred.stlouisfed.org/searchresults/?st=inflation+rate&isTst=1.

5 *How well have taxable investors been served in the 1980's and 1990's?* The Evidence-Based Investor. (n.d.). www.evidenceinvestor.com/evidence/well-taxable-investors-served-1980s-1990s/.

average index return. In fact, they will make you less! This is not because they are not intelligent people; an index fund has a lot less turnover when buying and selling stocks. Financial advisors do a great job of buying and selling stocks, but the price to pay for that is a killer cut to investors' returns. Each transaction leads to fees and costs associated.

We have explored some critical insights on why index investing has historically been a great place to put your money as a typical investor. Next, let us take a quick action step to help get the ball rolling on this process.

Chapter 3

It Is Time We Sat at a Computer

Core principle:
Action propels us to places we have never been.

There has almost certainly been a time in your life when you were given excellent advice, did not listen to it, and regretted it later down the road. Bobby gave me invaluable advice many years ago. I sat on the sideline for two years, frozen with fear of how to implement it. All I had to do was text Bobby and ask for help, which I finally did years later.

The hardest part of anything is getting started. Tiny steps forward make the task seem smaller and more manageable. Let us take our first small step.

I have always been passionate about motivation. This carries over to my career as a behavioral economist. I am still preaching action. I preached this action to my brother, and I am going to preach it to you. By taking this step, you are 57% more likely to start some sort of passively invested account.

OK, that is not true. That was the one and only false statistic in this book. Still, by understanding the basics of index funds, you are now starting to realize that little percentages like 5% can mean the difference between retiring financially independent and *your advisor* retiring financially independent. It can mean the difference between being able to pay for your child's education versus them having to take out loans. Action propels us into places we have never been. Now, it may not be 57%, but by taking small, actionable steps, you are more likely to succeed in the end than by taking a big, leaping step. Thus, I will encourage you to take these small steps with me along the way. Action helps bridge the gap between the person we are and the person we want to be.

Next, let us start to take some small actionable steps in the right direction. No investing will happen yet, and there is no cost involved in starting this process. This step is for you to get your feet wet. If it sounds overwhelming and scary, do not worry: It is important to note that following the steps in this book does not mean pouring all of your funds from your account into index funds. That is an option, but not the only option.

Amazing websites like Schwab.com allow the investor to invest with a minimum of $1 per fund! You could always test these methods with under $100 totally invested and see how you feel. If things feel right, then moving all your money over is an option.

This is not an attempt to pressure you into giving your money to some firm; instead, I am illustrating that index investing can help you save money. Otherwise, that money would be lost to fees and turnover if it were to be actively invested with an advisor or invested in individual stocks.

Action

I told my brother to look into brokerage houses like Schwab, Fidelity, Vanguard, etc.[6] These are not the only three places to house your accounts. Doing light research can tell you which one will offer you the best flexibility given your circumstances. I told Adam I house my money at Schwab. For now, I will focus on that particular brokerage house. However, it is essential to

6 For information on the top five most well-known brokerage houses in the US, visit Ross, S. (2022, February 8). *The biggest stock brokerages in the US*. Investopedia. www.investopedia.com/articles/professionals/110415/biggest-stock-brokerage-firms-us.asp'.

remember that similar firms like Fidelity, Vanguard, and many others offer similar platforms, mutual funds, and stock and bond options. Picking a place to house your money is simply based on your personal situation. When I started investing, my position was primarily characterized by not having a lot of money. This made Schwab a great fit because they have very low minimums. Schwab was also very intuitive, and I had a brick-and-mortar Schwab store five minutes from my house.

I will give you the same advice I gave my brother, verbatim: I invest with Schwab because I started with $25 a month. Again, Schwab is excellent for low minimum investing, and there was a store close by if I had any questions. Remember, you need no more than $1 per fund to start investing with Schwab. It is also not necessary to invest regularly each month. Doing so is advantageous, but not everyone can do so.

This is a small but actionable step. Most firms offer free accounts. It is crucial to make sure you find an reliable and reputable firm. The account may take up to a few days to be verified and linked.

Schwab vs. Fidelity vs. Vanguard

You likely still have some questions about the brokerage houses. Picking a place to house your money is no small decision. All of the firms offer various account types like brokerage, Roth IRA, Traditional IRA, trust, 529, etc. All of them provide no mutual fund trading costs. There is no minimum deposit for Fidelity or Schwab, and there is a $3,000 minimum for Vanguard. All of their websites are relatively simple and intuitive to use and maneuver.

The three brokerage houses we're focusing on are similar but not identical. Vanguard is known to be the originator in index funds, and Fidelity has a variety of educational features. While other websites have plenty of information, Fidelity offers tangible informational advantages to other firms. Schwab is known for its low investment minimums and provides a unique and accessible platform that helps you find low-cost funds based on a survey. Also, Schwab banking uses no-fee ATMs.

In the end, few differences set them apart; for the most part, each firm offers somewhat similar products and fees on a parallel scale. Some facets of a firm are probably more important to you than others. Doing some research will guide you to the best brokerage house for your situation and priorities.

As a disclaimer, please know that I am not affiliated with any of these brokerage houses. I do not care which one you choose. You should choose one that fits your needs the best. Talking to neighbors, friends, and family can be a great place to start. All the large firms are relatively identical, with few differentiable factors. Choosing one should not take too much thought or research. Again, if you are just starting, Schwab may be a great place because of their low minimums to start investing.

The important thing is to take time to seriously consider different firms. If you genuinely do not have a preference, in the end, having an account set up is much more critical than being paralyzed with indecision. Do not allow yourself to become stuck choosing between two large, reputable firms.

To recap, if you do care, choosing a firm that works best for your situation is essential. If you are a small investor like me, Vanguard's $3,000 minimum may not be the smartest choice. It would be vital for you to prioritize lower minimums. If you have an ample amount to invest, you might instead prioritize things like their website's simplicity, the firm's reputation, or their customer service. Everyone is in a unique situation; maximize yours. Remember, indecision is still an action.

Chapter 4
2 * 2 = 5

Core principle:
Compound interest is your best friend you have never met, but most friendships take time.

One day, I was walking around the beautiful campus of the University of Alabama (Roll Tide!). My first year of graduate school was in the books! I felt like I had finally made it. I was on my way to becoming the behavioral economist I have always wanted to be.

It was a beautiful day on the quad. I was out for a mid-morning walk when my brother called. I remember our conversation vividly because I walked from the quad to sorority row to the stadium multiple times.

My brother started throwing a multitude of math equations at me. He asked me if someone invests $100,000 at the market return of 10% for 10 years and they only make $100,000 in returns, how can people get so rich using the stock market?

The first point I made was that the stock market is not made for getting rich quick. If you want that, then stop talking to me and go ask a psychic. The second thing I told him was that he was forgetting about the crucial concept of compound interest.

He asked me what compound interest is, and I told him it is like multiplying 2 * 2 and getting 5—but only if you let it grow.

I took his example and flipped it on its head: Assume we are using a 10% interest rate each year and an initial investment of $100,000. The difference between simple and compound interest is critical to understand. In a scenario where your $100,000 is earning simple interest, your initial investment is multiplied by each year's interest rate. Compound interest multiplies your initial investment and the cumulative interest you have made in any previous years by the interest rate. Let us look at this scenario in a chart:

Year	Simple interest revenue for each year total	Compound interest revenue for each year total
1	$100,000 * 10% = $10,000	$100,000 * 10% = $10,000
2	$100,000 * 10% = $10,000	$110,000 * 10% = $11,000
3	$100,000 * 10% = $10,000	$121,000 * 10% = $12,100
4	$100,000 * 10% = $10,000	$133,100 * 10% = $13,310
5	$100,000 * 10% = $10,000	$146,410 * 10% = $14,641
:	:	:
9	$100,000 * 10% = $10,000	$214,358.88 * 10% = $21,435.89
10	$100,000 * 10% = $10,000	$235,794.77 * 10% = $23,579.48
Total interest revenue	$100,000	$159,374.25

After 10 years and a 10% return, I showed Adam that you could have close to $60,000 more in the bank when compound interest is allowed to happen. I told him the magic of compound interest is that the past returns are included in next year's principle (or the amount that the 10% return works on). In other words, your interest revenue from *last* year makes you money *this* year. This may not seem like much, but after years and years, those extra dollars add up.

After this simple 10-year example, the compound interest return column has about 60% more money. Investing in any capacity, not just index funds, gives the investor the incredible advantage of compound interest.

He liked when I used dollar figures, but he still had a hard time comprehending the idea of compound interest. Therefore, I followed that example with a more straightforward illustration of how compounding works. Simple, yet profound. The math can be strange, but you should know compound interest is always working for you when using the market.

Let us say you take a penny and double the amount you have every day for a month. How much money do you think you will have at the end of the 30 days? Take a guess before you look at the number.

$50?

.

.

.

$1,000?

.

.

.

You are thinking it is a trick. What then? $100,000?

.

.

.

Try $5,368,709.12! That is the power of compounding. Your money builds on itself. Compounding interest is truly a powerful financial opportunity. Even if you do not fully understand or comprehend it, it will work for you no matter what type of investment you are invested in. It even works against you; just look at how some people can get into the tens of thousands of credit card debt.

Nevertheless, compounding only works its wonders when you have time and consistency on your hands. Compounding will do next to nothing for your portfolio if you only have one or two years to invest.

I told my brother that since he is young and can invest, he needs to start now. No matter your age, the sooner you start investing, the sooner compound interest will work for you.

Let us say two individuals are both 30 years old and plan to retire at 65. One is named Zack, and the other is named Adam. Adam is smart and starts investing right away with the $1,000 he has. He decides to contribute $100 a month to the fund until he is 65.

On the other hand, Zack naively feels that it is not the right time to get into the market and waits until 40 to start investing. At 40, Zack invests $1,000 and contributes $100 a month until he is 65.

Let us see who has accrued more money when they turn 65: Adam, who started as soon as possible, or Zack, who "timed" the market. For this example, I will set the return at 10%, close to the stock market's average return. Also, the money will be compounded monthly.

	Zack	**Adam**
Total years invested	25	35
Contribution each month after initial $1,000 investment	$100	$100
Total amount invested	$31,000	$43,000
Amount for retirement	$145,845.98	$415,466.32

Adam ends up with close to three times the amount Zack does. Zack waited 10 years to start investing for retirement and lost out on $269,620.34. In a sense, Zack lost out on over $250,000 for the price of $12,000 less invested.

Those that think the stock market will continue to average close to what it has in its entire existence, want to invest for the mid to long term, and have the benefit of time on their hands should invest as soon as possible. No one has been able to time the market; thus, the best time to start investing is NOW.

This particular example resonated with my brother, and he finally let me sit down with him and open an account to start his investing career.

In the end, compound interest may be the best friend you have never met, and it will always be there for you. Compound interest has extraordinary power, and you do not have to do anything for it to work for you. It is important to remember that time is the crux to that power. It is not necessary to understand absolutely everything about compound interest; just know its influence on your portfolio.

Chapter 5

Now vs. Later Investing

Core principle:
If you can do it, DO. IT. NOW.

My brother told me he did not see a point in investing right now because he only had $25 to spare each month. Investing is a slow-moving process. If you only have 2% of your income to invest, do it anyway! Slowly try to start investing more and more. Remember, I just showed you how those tiny percentages could add up. Time is one of the most important aspects of compounding; the sooner you start, the sooner compounding starts to work for you. Drink one less coffee a week from Starbucks, bring your lunch one more day, or carpool to work a few days a month.

Let us look at a quick example of investing early versus later when you have more money:

	Alice	**Beth**	**Jessica**
Start age for retirement contributions	25	45	55
Retirement age	65	65	65
Monthly contribution	$20	$40	One deposit of $9,600

Total amount contributed	$9,600	$9,600	$9,600
End portfolio value	$127,535.60	$30,627.88	$25, 987.60

In this example, the return rate was set at 10%, compounded monthly. All three women retire at 65 and contribute the same amount of money, but Alice started early and ended up with a little over four times the amount Beth did in the end.

Time is your best friend in investing. If you have time on your hands but not much to invest, INVEST ANYWAY. It will add up over time. Maybe not to millions, but much more than if you did not invest at all.

Here is a hard truth: You will need to give up some short-term pleasures for long-term financial success. This is a tricky thing to do. There is a powerful temptation to splurge on that $5 Starbucks coffee or $7 blk water. However, if you can find the extra $20 a month, your future self will thank you. Whom do you want to be like in the future? Alice? Or Jessica?

Choosing long-term success over short-term gratification is a struggle for everyone. If you have a problem cutting back on a coffee or lunch each week, start by picking up a side hustle and using that money to invest. There are great companies out there that let you make money on your time and terms—Uber, Lyft, Amazon Mechanical Turk, etc. Slowly bump that number up as time goes on. It will pay dividends. Literally.

Chapter 6

No, No, No, You Cannot Time the Market Either

Core principle:

Staying invested is the easiest way to stay ahead.

The very next week, Adam called me and said, "I am starting to understand this stuff you have been telling me, but what's stopping me from pulling all my money out when a recession is about to hit? I would lose out on the bad years and make a lot more than 10% return!" I answered him with this illustration.

Let us suppose Zack and Adam both invest simultaneously, but Zack likes to pull his money out of the market when things get tough and the market is dropping fast. Therefore, he thinks he is losing less money than Adam is. But this is only true in the short term.

For example's sake, we will say that Zack does not reinvest for another year while the market recovers. Let us look at the numbers. Both Zack and Adam initially contributed $100,000 as well as an additional monthly sum of $200.

Year	Zack's interest rate for the year	Zack's year-end portfolio value	Adam's interest rate for the year	Adam's year-end portfolio value
1	15%	$118,679.67	15%	$118,679.67
2	4%	$125,967.50	4%	$125,967.50
3	-13%	$112,770.59	-26%	$98,937.70
4	0%	$112,770.59	42%	$152,524.26
5	6%	$122,205.48	6%	$164,411.07
6	-5%	$118,569.29	-5%	$158,712.29
7	18%	$144,410.96	18%	$192,406.66
8	2%	$149,751.96	2%	$198,716.42
9	-25%	$118,417.93	-37%	$156,450.91
10	0%	$118,417.93	69%	$309,531.27
Average	.2%		8.8%	
Total		$118,417.93		$309,531.27

Like most people, Zack was fearful of a significant market correction, but he missed huge upswings in the market because of his fear. Interestingly, the market's most considerable upswings have historically happened after these market corrections.

Look at the example: By staying fully invested through the market downturns, one would yield around an 8 to 9% return on average. In the example above, Zack missed a year of investing because of his fear. This means he missed out on some of the market's most significant upswings. In fact, missing just the top 30 performing days will yield a portfolio of less than 1% on average. Compare that to the S&P 500's typical return of 10%.

By pulling his money out of the market in a downturn, Zack may have lost out on a short-term loss. However, the long-term effects of this are devastating. This will not allow Zack to stay in front of inflation either. He could have returned more on average by merely investing in a safer vehicle with less fluctuation if risk makes him want to pull his money out of the market.

I do not blame my brother for thinking he could time the market. However, it is critical to understand that it is virtually impossible. Those investors who miss part or all of the downturn also typically miss the market's next upturn. Moreover, if an investor did manage to miss much of the downturn, they would still need to put their money back in at the "right" time to gain from the market during its most prosperous times (which are historically after downturns).

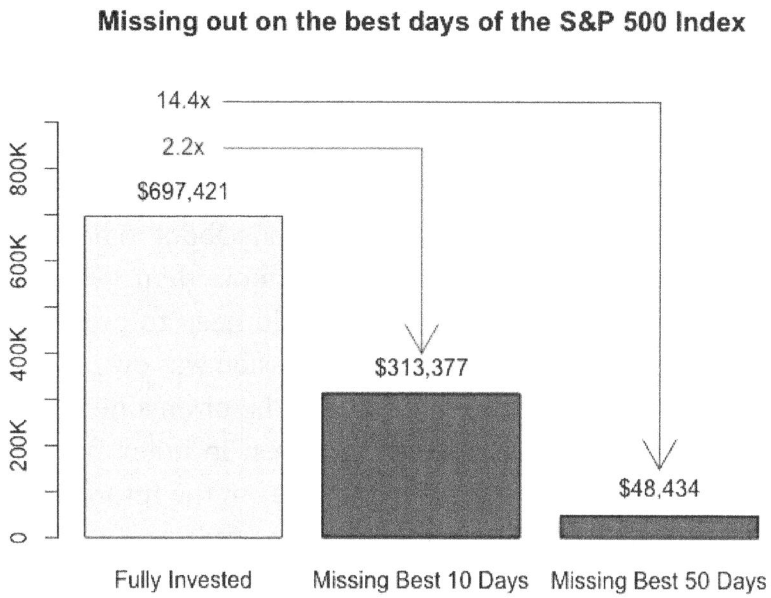

According to Fidelity[7], if we hypothetically had $10,000 invested in the S&P 500 Index from January 1, 1980, to March 31, 2020, missing even the 10 best days of the market could be devastating to our return. If all we invested was $10,000 and let it grow for 40 years and did not miss any days, we would yield close to $700,000.

Now, if we missed the best 10 days trying to time the market, we could only end up with close to $313,000. That $313,000

7 *Don't miss best days - fidelity investments*. (n.d.). Retrieved March 12, 2022, from www.fidelity.com/bin-public/060_www_fidelity_com/documents/dont-miss-best-days.pdf.

would be 2.2 times smaller than the case in which we stayed fully invested. Alternatively, if we missed the best 50 days trying to time the market, we could only end up with close to $50,000. That $50,000 would be 14.4 times smaller than the case in which we stayed fully invested. If you tried to time the market and, by chance, missed a measly 50 out of 14,600 days over 40 years, you would not only just barely stay above inflation, but you would also yield close to $650,000 less than if you just stayed invested.

In a little bit, we will touch more on this and explore how trying to time the market like this can be a chore with devastating consequences for every ill call. In the next chapter, we will cover corrections and how the market has responded to them in the past.

Let's return to my brother's question: "What's stopping me from pulling all my money out when a recession is about to hit? I would lose out on the bad years and make a lot more than 10% return." For Adam to do this successfully, he would need to predict when the recession would hit and when the recession was over. He would need to do so with incredible accuracy. If he or anyone else could forecast a recession, they should not invest in index funds; they should start putting all their money on bets in the future direction of the stock market. The fact is no one can predict recessions with 100% accuracy. What makes you think you can?

Here is a fun game to play if you think you can time the market: Start with 10 shares of Bama stock, each worth $100. Go 30 periods. Each period, you can choose to stay invested, or you can pay $15 per share to sell any or all of your shares at the current price. Flip a coin each period, which determines if the stock goes up $5 or down $5. Heads it goes up; tails it goes down. See if you can make more money than a player who remains invested for the entire 30 periods.

To make this clear, say it is the fifth period, and the current stock price is $125. You can sell all 10 of your shares and have $1250 - $150 = $1100 cash to buy back in when you want. You need to beat whatever the end stock price is, times 10 shares. It is a fun game to play, and you might even be able to beat it. But can you beat it repeatedly?

Nevertheless, the trick is you would need to beat it consistently to have any skin in the game to time the market. Most people think they can beat statistics. This simple game demonstrates why it is more challenging than it looks.

The moral of the story is that if you want to produce any type of significant returns, you need to let the power of time, compound interest, and the mental fortitude to stay invested drive that boat for you. Every time you want to pull your money out because you think we are in for a crash, go ahead and play my silly little coin flipping game before you do. Timing the market is as futile as trying to beat the flipping of a coin. In the end, staying invested is the best way to stay ahead in your returns.

Chapter 7

If You Want to Be a Fortune Teller, You Had Better Be a Damn Good One

Core Principle:

Keep fear in check. It is easy to be overwhelmed by fear. If we understand where anxiety comes from, we can lessen it. Some fears are irrational, but fearing market downturns is not one of them.

Bad financial events will happen. At some point, we must assume that they will. This is not meant to scare you but to inform you of their frequency. These downturns in the market are often referred to as bear markets.

This term scares many people, like my brother, but I told him that he should not be. I asked him if he would still be frightened if he could know that he would come out the other side better off than he was before.

I challenged him with an example: Suppose your employer took a random percentage out of your paycheck every year. You would likely fear that they would take out so much you could not pay your bills. But what if you knew that your employer would eventually give you back that money they took, and most times give you more than they took? Your fear would not be gone entirely, but you would probably be more at ease with that information. Corrections and bear markets have historically worked similarly.

This example did not click with my brother. Using the S&P 500 returns according to CNBC,[8] I showed him what happened after some of the most horrific downturns in the stock market.

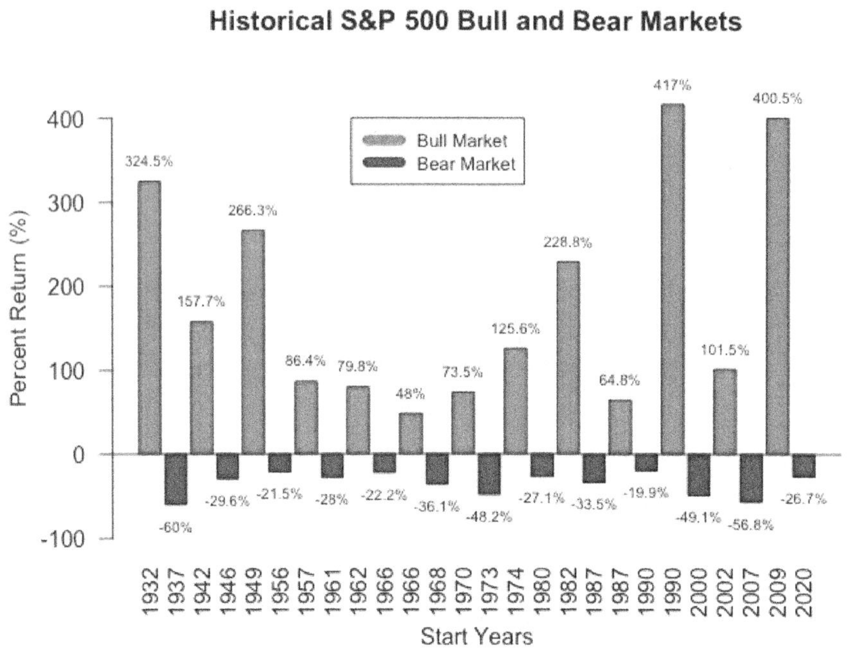

What do you notice happened after almost every bear market we have ever had? A bull market (where prices are on the rise) typically follows, with percent increases as high as 417%.

Therefore, maybe you are like Zack in my last example and can pull your money out before the bear market eats you alive. BUT, like the chart in the previous chapter showed, if you miss the top 50 days, which typically occur after a bear market, you can lose out on most to all of your potential return.

8 Tomwfranck. (2020, March 14). *A look at Bear and bull markets through history.* CNBC. Retrieved March 11, 2022, from https://www.cnbc.com/2020/03/14/a-look-at-bear-and-bull-markets-through-history.html.

This process of putting your money in and taking it out is not as simple as it sounds; the best and simplest thing to do is stay invested to generate superior returns. By simplest, I purely mean least effort involved. You do not need to time the market. You do not need to consistently pull your money out and then figure out the best time to put it back in. The hardest part is watching your portfolio dip by 56.8% like it did in 2007.

The next thing everyone says, including my brother, is, "Zack, if the trend is there, shouldn't I use the direction to my advantage? Shouldn't I pull my money out before a big market dip and just put it back in when the market turns around?"

Keep these things in mind: What if everyone is calling for doomsday, and you pull all your money out? If the market skyrockets 100% the next day, you will lose money because you have to pay fees to leave your position and not benefit from the market upsurge. What if you successfully pulled your money out and you are waiting on the sidelines to reinvest, and suddenly the market starts to upsurge a little? You could put all your money back, but the market takes another dive.

Wherever you get your stock market news, I promise you they will wrongly predict the sky is falling far more often than they are right. No financial analyst has over 20 years in financial analysis and has even close to a 100% accuracy level for predicting the markets' movements. If you cannot trust financial analysts, who do you trust to tell you how to time the market?

Trick question: YOU DO NOT TIME THE MARKET! Plain and simple. If you want to time the market, Adam, let us talk about how often you have to be prepared to do it.

Correction vs. Bear Market

Let us define the terms correction and bear market. This will give you an idea of how often you have to correctly time the market if you choose to go that route instead of staying invested. This knowledge will provide you with some peace of mind next time a downturn occurs.

A market correction = A decline of 10% or more in the price of the market

A bear market = A decline of 20% or more in the price of the market

How often do these events occur? Well, for a correction, an investor would have to try to time that at least once a year, on average. How about a bear market? Those would have to be timed every three to five years, on average. Please reread those two last sentences. Although these statistics are very informative, I do not think that you can use them to predict the market's future behavior. Just because the market is "due" for a correction or bear market does not mean it will happen precisely when scheduled. These events occur only on average every year and every three to five years, respectively.

Here is the good news: If you stay invested and have listened to the words I have said, you should expect, on average, to return around 10% in index funds. You will not have to time the market, which could involve pulling your money out EVERY year. Moreover, less than 20% of all market corrections turn into bear markets. No one, not even Warren Buffet, can time the market. The beauty of staying invested and investing in the mid to long term is that you should not even really care if a correction is going to turn into a bear market or not. This is because you KNOW they have happened, and they will happen again. Take comfort that over the long haul, the bull markets have overshadowed the bear markets.

Here's some advice, because you have heard the horror stories once and you'll hear them again and again: Stop listening to the so-called "experts" on the stock market. They predict that almost every market correction will turn into a bear market. Turn off CNBC, Bloomberg, etc. You now have knowledge about how the market statistically operates. It has been proven that over time, the stock market is on an increasing linear trend. So, read my words again and again. Stay invested. Stay the course. Stop listening to "experts" that do not know what they are talking about. Stop listening to your neighbor. Read the facts of the past few graphs.

Recency Bias

As a behavioral economist, I would be remiss if I did not share a bias that we all have. These "experts" are not trying to scare you on purpose. They are merely stuck believing the sky is falling. Recency bias is like a meter in our head that tells us that what has happened recently will continue to happen forever.

A perfect example of this is having a cold or flu that you thought would never end. You believed this cold would continue forever because it had not let up in five days. Alternatively, maybe you thought that you would be stuck with the pain of heartbreak forever and would never get over it. Humans tend to believe that the most recent thing that has happened will continue forever.

This works for positive events as well. When the stock market is going up, people think it will go up forever. When people are on a hot streak, they think it will never end.

When the market is correcting, we always believe we are in for another bear market. This leads us to make silly, foolish errors and even broadcast them for all to see. They say hindsight is 20/20; let this book be your hindsight for every correction and bear market to come. Stay invested. Because during the next market correction, you better believe that everyone, including the experts, is going to tell you that the sky is falling. However, now you are equipped with the knowledge that only 20% of corrections turn into a bear market. What is the most important thing you can do?

Keep your fear in check.

If you pull your money out of the market, you are risking losing most of your potential return. If you can keep fear in check, you will not need to think about pulling your money out. The knowledge you have will allow you to rest easy.

In the next chapter, we will talk about how much an active advisor is costing you and how much you can save by transferring your money to a passive account (over 133 times less than an active account). Again, we all can start small. Doing all this at once can seem daunting and scary. If starting small is the key to success for you, only contribute small amounts until you get comfortable with the process, website, and concepts I teach. Once this happens, you can slowly move more and more money.

My brother loves to check the stock market, and so did I when I was actively investing. Now, I rarely check it. The only time I check it is when the market is declining. I do not check it because a declining market scares me. Instead, I know I can get stocks on sale when that is happening, and I buy more. I made my brother put a Post-it on his mirror that says in large letters, "STAY INVESTED, STAY LOGGED OFF, AND DO NOT RELIGIOUSLY LISTEN TO THEM." My brother is on his way to becoming a better, more educated financial investor, but first, he needs to understand how much his financial advisor is costing him.

Chapter 8

Passive vs. Active Investing

Core Principle:

You can either be ignorant and end up the fool or become educated and end up the sage.

Before I explained to Adam what passive and active investing are, I asked my brother what he would do in this scenario:

Say you are a farmer with little experience and a small farm and have three options for plowing your crop. The first option is your trusted automatic plow. It allows you to plow your field and pick up 70% of your crop with some work. The second option is your most preferred option: very skilled human pickers who can retrieve very close to 100% of your harvest for the year. The problem is they are costly, and you would need a much larger farm for that to be feasible. The third option is the average pickers who will come to your farm and tell you they have great techniques for retrieving a large amount of the crop. They will charge you less than the very skilled pickers in the second option (which you cannot afford), and they tell you they will be more efficient than the automatic plow. You research the average pickers, who have a new way to pick your crop and find they typically start out strong. However, over five to ten years, they average a yield of around

50% and cost over 20 times more than the gas and knowledge needed to run your automatic plow. Which option do you choose? One or three?

My brother answered my example by saying that if you have the knowledge that the new pickers will only average 50% of your crop, you would be stupid not to go with option one.

This farmer example illustrates the difference between using index funds to invest and paying an advisor to help you invest. In this same spirit, with "passive" investing, you can save thousands of dollars that slowly slip away through fees via "active" investing. *Passive* investing is investing in index funds, while *active* investing is investing with an advisor or buying and selling individual stocks.

First, let us state some facts:

1. The S&P 500 index has averaged around 10% return over the past 90 years.
2. Financial advisors have averaged their clients around 7% BEFORE fees.
3. Fees for financial advice can range from 1 to 3% of your portfolio each year.
4. Even when you make a negative return for a fiscal year, advisors still get their cut.
5. After advisor fees, investors have averaged around 5 to 6%.
6. Index fund yearly expense ratios average as low as **.015%**! (By the time you are reading this, they might be as low as 0.00%.)

Index funds will not only charge as low as .015%, but they also have also averaged close to 3 to 4% more than what a typical advisor has returned for their clients. Let us say your financial advisor charges you 2%. That 2% costs more than 133 times more than a passive account.

Since you now understand the powerful tool of compounding, I am sure you can see where this will go. Nevertheless, we will look into examples just for completeness. Remember, little percentages can grow into large sums when compounded over many years.

Your advisor wants to take 2% from your returns each year. That 2% number seems incredibly insignificant to many clients. Let us look at the potential actual dollar figures to that 2%.

Consider two investors: John and Fred. Neither John nor Fred has much money to invest in the market, but both are smart and start as soon as possible. At the age of 25, both John and Fred invest $1,000 and contribute $100 a month for their retirement until age 65. John decides to hire a financial advisor. His advisor charges him 2% each year on his portfolio. John averages 5% over 40 years. On the other hand, Fred has read *Get Off Your Ass and Invest* and decides to invest in index funds. He pays around .015% on his portfolio each year and averages 9.985% over 40 years.

	John - active investor	**Fred - passive investor**
Total years invested	40	40
Contribution each month after initial $1,000 investment	$100	$100
Interest rate	5%	9.985%
Total amount invested after 40 years	$49,000	$49,000
Amount for retirement	$160,596.27	$689,224.03

Fred ends up with close to four times the amount that John does, thanks to the power of compound interest. If you are interested in calculating similar figures that are more congruent with your finances, you can see this for yourself on a compound interest calculator easily found online.

Adam's eyes lit up when he saw these dollar figures, and then he made an incredibly insightful comment. He said, "Zack, those numbers seem so low to retire on." These numbers are rather low for what you would need to retire comfortably, so let us rerun them with the national averages. In this example, we have two average Joes: Joe Clerk and Joe Sales. Joe Clerk and Joe Sales both earn $60,000, the median house income in America.[9] Joe Clerk is an active investor, meaning he decides to hire a financial advisor, and his advisor charges him 2% each year. He averages 5% over 40 years. On the other hand, Joe Sales has read *Get Off Your Ass and Invest* and decides to invest in index funds. He has to pay around .015% on his portfolio each year and averages a return of 9.985% over 40 years.

It has been said that every investor should aim to be saving 20% of their income. In this case, 20% of $60,000 is $12,000. However, this is not reasonable for everyone, so let us see the numbers for someone who saves 5%, 10%, 15%, and 20%, respectively. For the exercise's sake, let us assume that Joe Clerk and Joe Sales cannot start investing until they are 35, even though the most important part of investing is starting as soon as possible, regardless of the amount. Both are flat broke and have nothing to contribute other than a certain percentage of their income broken up over 12 months.

Contribution = 5% of income		
Total years invested	30	30
Contribution each month	$250	$250
Interest rate	5%	9.985%
Amount for retirement	$208, 931.59	$568,612.53

Contribution = 10% of income		
Total years invested	30	30
Contribution each month	$500	$500
Interest rate	5%	9.985%
Amount for retirement	$417,863.19	$1,137,225.06

9 Bureau, U. S. C. (2021, October 18). *Income and poverty in the United States: 2019*. Census.gov. https://www.census.gov/library/publications/2020/demo/p60-270.html

Contribution = 15% of income		
Total years invested	30	30
Contribution each month	$750	$750
Interest rate	5%	9.985%
Amount for retirement	$626,794.78	$1,705,837.59

Contribution = 20% of income		
Total years invested	30	30
Contribution each month	$1,000	$1,000
Interest rate	5%	9.985%
Amount for retirement	$835,726.38	$2,274,450.12

When I showed this to my brother, his eyes lit up like a Christmas tree. It is important to remember that this is a dramatic example illustrating the vast differences "little" percentages each year make on a portfolio. These are examples of portfolios that are invested 100% in stocks without any risk management with bonds. While this may look like a great idea, an investor also needs to minimize risks associated with the stock market by investing in bonds, like index bonds. We will talk more about this idea in chapter 10 when we explore the concept of allocation.

Tiny percentages add up to large numbers. The numbers in the examples above are not perfect fortune tellers, but if you stay invested with an active financial advisor, you could be leaving hundreds of thousands of dollars on the table. To be more precise, those dollars will slowly slip from the table into the management firm and manager's pocket over the years. Adam was starting to realize why financial advisors tell you they take 2% of your returns and not show you the real dollar figures behind those percentages. The math is the same. Just the information is displayed in two different ways.

Nevertheless, explaining anything in dollar figures always seems to capture everyone's attention. If you don't comprehend the numbers, then simply ask yourself, "When I retire, do I want

$835,726.38 or $2,274,450.1251 to live off of?" That should be a pretty easy decision. It is your decision to choose active or passive investing.

Remember this: Even when you make a negative return for a fiscal year, advisors still get their cut. You pay your advisor 2% of your portfolio each year to help you make a decision, and even in a negative return year, an advisor will still take 2% of your portfolio. Of course, the same thing will happen for index funds, but it will be a drastically smaller number coming out of your portfolio. If you do well, your advisor does well. If you do poorly, your advisor will still expect to be paid.

Hopefully, like my brother, you would be the farmer who would invest in knowledge and choose to pick the automatic plow/index funds, which can average a better and cheaper crop yield/return. Once someone has the information, there is little reason to choose option three, the average pickers. The average pickers are a poor decision, and there is little reason to hire an advisor who cannot beat an index return, on average.

Chapter 9

New Weeds in the Grass

Core Principle:
A dollar here, a dollar there, everyone gets a dollar. Just because something is new does not automatically mean it is better.

I feel this chapter will become increasingly relevant in the present financial market. While researching, my brother ran into new firms springing up, promising commission-free trading. They are called financial technology, or fintech, companies. They use emerging technology to compete with the older, larger, and more established financial firms.

Before thinking about investing with these firms, one should be aware of how these firms make money. An investment firm, or a capitalistic firm in general, needs to make money in some way to stay profitable and afloat. These firms can make money in various ways: taking pennies off a rounded-up investment; making money on premium accounts, lending interest, or high-frequency trading; or investing the cash currently sitting in your account but not invested. This is similar to how banks can stay profitable.

It is essential to know how these firms are taking their share of "commission-free" trading. You have now learned that little two percentages can have devastating effects on the end value of a portfolio. You must now understand that pennies off each dollar work the same way. This new form of trading takes those two percentages in a new (perhaps more devastating) path to your portfolio.

These Fintech companies are very appealing to younger generations. Why? They promise to invest small sums of your money for small membership fees. When I heard commission-free trading and $1-per-month fees for the first time, I was excited too. That was, at least, until I did the math. The truth is these new companies are just trying to capture the new generation of people who do not have trust in the financial sector. They are doing the same thing as active managers but in a much sneakier way.

However, not all fintech companies are created equal. First, you need to know how you are being charged. Then you need to do the math.

What is the best thing to do when the numbers seem unclear? An example! The numbers below are close to realistic numbers reported for a real fintech company in recent years.

The first thing to know is how much you are being charged. The membership fee from a firm I researched was $1.25 per month, or $15 a year. Not bad. Let us look at three scenarios and see how much $15 a year is really costing us.

Scenario 1: You have $100 invested with this fintech company, and you returned 10% this year. Your return before fees is $10. If you paid $15 for membership fees, you would end up reducing your $100 principle to $95. You would make a negative return after those “cheap” $1.25 monthly payments.

Scenario 2: You have $500 invested with this Fintech company, and you returned 10% this year. Your return before fees is $50. If you paid $15 for membership fees, you would end up with a 7% return.

Scenario 3: You have $100,000 invested with this Fintech company, and you returned 10% this year. Your return before fees is $100,000. If you paid $15 for membership fees, you would yield close to a 9.985% return. This means you would need $100,000 invested to be anywhere near the index fund ratio of .015%.

"Small" fees will eat you alive. Run the numbers for yourself. How much would you need to return each year for that yearly fee percentage to be near the index fund expense ratio of .015%? In other words, how much would you have to invest with one of these firms for the cost to equal the yearly price of investing in an index fund?

So much for helping people with small amounts of money invest without being robbed! Some of these companies offer free commission trading without account costs, but you should be conscious of the available options. Some of these fintech companies do not offer mutual funds, bonds, or retirement account options.

Be aware of the sharks in the deep end and those lurking in the shallow end. Those tend to be the deadliest! These new firms see you covering your pockets, and they still swipe the money from right under your feet. The financial services market is brilliant and very good at what it does. These are businesses that are run for profit, so they are very good at extracting all the money they can from investors. As a percentage of the population, fewer and fewer people are investing long term in the stock market. I would hypothesize that this is due to a lack of information combined with a lack of trust in the financial system. This has led to these new and ingenious ways being created to lure more people into investing.

To speak my brother's language again, $1 a month feels like an astronomically small number to spend each month. Nevertheless, this is the new and sneaky way from the financial sector to extract those tiny two percentages.

If you do not care to learn how a company earns its profit from you, stay with companies who are very straightforward about charging you. Do not go out looking for a "deal" when picking a financial house to invest in. If you cannot explain how floats work and how companies use them to make money off you, do not use them. If you cannot confidently explain how a fintech company you invest with makes money off you, do not use it. Remember, every capitalistic firm needs to earn profit to survive.

I cannot stress enough that when you first start investing, losing pennies on the dollar can be devastating to allow compounding to work its magic. Commission-free trading, which is now becoming available to larger firms mentioned in past chapters, and $1-per-month fees sound great, but most don't understand the mathematical implications. Now you do. Dollars have a way of adding up to unexpectedly large numbers. Take the concept of buying a $3.29 cup of coffee each morning before work. That coffee, which could be made at home for pennies on the dollar, has added up to cost you close to $1,000 a year.

Chapter 10

Allocation

Core Principle:

You and I might end the race in the same place but run very different routes to get there.

The way your portfolio is broken down is called its allocation. Basically, an allocation answers the question "What kind of and how many stocks and bonds do I have?" What percentage of my portfolio is held in stocks? What percentage is held in bonds? This can be broken down even further by defining how you want to break down those stocks. For instance, my portfolio might consist of 30% bonds and 70% stocks. In this example, let's suppose all 30% of the bonds I hold are aggregate index bonds. Of the 70% of my portfolio invested in stocks, I might have 20% invested in US index funds, 20% in foreign index funds, and 30% in total index funds. This is merely an example allocation. You will have to find one that is ideal for you and your financial situation.

I cannot advise you on what sort of allocation is perfect for you. My brother wanted me to tell him exactly what kind of allocation is ideal, but that is not how this works. The truth is, choosing an allocation is a complicated question that may take some personal pondering before you are ready to act.

I told my brother to think of an allocation like deciding a college major. If one person wants to be a doctor and one person wants to be an electrician, they will choose drastically different majors and most likely will not attend the same institution to learn their craft. Someone who values job security most might work in something like engineering, accounting, or finance. Someone who values expressing themselves through their work might work as an actor, artist, or musician. Again, both will major in very different departments. Everyone wants to be happy and have a promising career, but the way they choose to get there can be contingent on purpose, risk, and time horizon. This is just like picking an allocation.

Let us first discuss the most important things to keep in mind when picking an allocation that works with your unique situation and preferences.

1. First and most important, what is your purpose for investing? It is essential to know what you would like to achieve in each of your accounts. What is it you are trying to accomplish with the account? Basically, what do you hope to use the money for? How much time do you have? What are the restrictions on the account?
2. Next, how risky of an investor are you? Are you one to squirm when the market is taking a severe downturn? If you are, more bonds and other safe investments may be crucial to staying the course. Do you have a longer time frame to invest over? If you do, risk will be minimized by that long period of being in the market. A higher stock percentage in your allocation will maximize your profits and capitalize on your time horizon.
3. What percent should be devoted to bonds and safer assets? What percentage should be dedicated to stocks and riskier assets? One popular solution is to carry your age in bonds. Meaning when you are 20, hold 20% bonds and 80% stocks. When you turn 30, sell 10% of your stocks and buy 10% more bonds, so your ratio now becomes 30% bonds and 70%

stocks. This makes the most sense for retirement investing because as you get closer to distributing your funds, you will want to have a higher bond ratio to mitigate the risk associated with stocks. This is not a perfect solution but more of a helpful guideline. There are many more methodologies out there. It is crucial to answer the first two questions, and then the third will be easier to break down.

Answering these three questions will help you immensely when picking an allocation. You might want to ask yourself these questions for each account you have set up, as they will likely have different goals.

There are a few key concepts here that are critical to understanding. If you have a more extended time period to invest, then having a higher stock percent of your portfolio is OK. If you have a shorter investment horizon, then having more bonds helps mitigate the risk associated with shorter-term investing. If you like risk and can tolerate significant fluctuations in return each year (even negative ones), having more equities is OK. If you are averse to risk, then an allocation that contains more bonds may help you stay the course and stay invested, even when you are losing money during a correction or bear market. It is vital to select an allocation that makes you feel secure. It would be counterproductive to have a portfolio that scares you and causes you to pull your money out of the market during downturns. For example, bonds lead to less loss in ebb periods and less gain in the flow periods. If that minimization of loss in the ebb periods is needed for peace of mind, factor that into your allocation.

We talked earlier about careers and their similarities to allocations. You might choose to go into a career that is more lucrative and riskier. On the other hand, you might decide to go into a safer job that makes you happy and compensates you less. It is OK to pursue a career that will not make you a multimillionaire. In this same vein, you can pick an allocation that is not money maximizing. Meaning, if a safer allocation (like more weight in bonds) makes you sleep better at night, then that might be the perfect allocation for you. There is no ideal allocation for everyone because everyone has different emotions, risk levels, ages, time horizons, end goals, etc.

Change Is OK!

When time horizons are small or approaching the period of your life when you will be withdrawing from your accounts, allocation becomes very important. When it is time for you to start withdrawing some or all of your funds, it is crucial to be invested more heavily in bonds to mitigate the short-term risk associated with the market. Bonds minimize the risk because stocks are more volatile investments—meaning they have typically had higher highs and lower lows than bonds. Therefore, if you are heavily invested in stocks a few years away from retirement and the stock market takes a 50% drop in value, you will not be able to retire on time, possibly spending another handful of years trying to get back to where you once were. Later, we will explore in greater detail rebalancing your portfolio as your age or situation changes.

This decision is not an easy one to make. It is essential to take the time to reflect on what sort of allocation works best for your brokerage and/or your retirement account. How much of my portfolio should be composed of stocks? Bonds? It is OK if these percentages are different for your different accounts. Asking friends may also help you understand what others do for your given age, time horizon, and situation.

The best news is that you will not be wed to this allocation. It can easily be changed over time. We are all looking to get to the promised land of financial freedom, but the path we all take there might be drastically different, and that is OK. Your age, time horizon, risk preferences, and goals will help you pick an allocation and change that allocation according.

Short-, Mid-, and Long-Term Investing

When making an allocation, it is also important to keep three buckets in mind: short, mid, and long term. Short term can be anywhere from tomorrow to around a year and a half to two years in the future. It is essential to keep enough cash reserves to fund your daily life and some extra in case of emergencies in the short term.

Long term is associated with retirement. We want to make sure we are allocating sufficient funds to our retirement accounts to retire on time for the long term. Allocating your age in bonds is more geared toward long-term investing.

Mid-term is anywhere between short and long term. For the mid-term, we want to be using a brokerage account to do our investing. This is where time horizon and risk levels are variable for most people. Mid-term investing will take the most thought.

Chapter 11

90/10 Principle

Core Principle:

There is nothing wrong with buying an individual stock. Just do not let it overshadow your portfolio or end goal.

My brother and I loved driving from our home in Buffalo, New York, to Erie, Pennsylvania, to grab some Chick-fil-A, Krispy Kreme, and Steak n' Shake. The drive was only about an hour, and most times, it was more about spending time in the car than actually eating at the restaurants. We would typically do it after a semester to celebrate our hard work and accomplishments.

One particular time, my brother invited a bunch of his friends. I remember this drive specifically because they all kept going on and on about Bitcoin. Let me be clear: I am not, nor will I ever, give advice on which stocks to pick or not pick. Instead, I want to discuss a particular conversation from that night.

Adam's friend was talking about how he had made $200 using Bitcoin. Another one of his friends was so interested in Bitcoin after the conversation that he told us he would invest $5,000 into Bitcoin the next day. The next day, my brother asked my advice whether he should invest in Bitcoin or not. Instinctively, I said no. In the end, he invested anyway and lost a significant amount of money. I was very disturbed by the whole situation, so like many times when I was confused, I called Bobby.

I told him about my ride to Erie the previous day. The first question out of my mouth was, "Bobby, is there ever any room for individual stocks in a portfolio?" He said, "Of course, if you want there to be." I was confused because I thought the books I had been reading, the conversations I had been having, and the research I had been doing were all advising against actively investing.

Bobby said, "If you want to invest all your money in index funds, great. If you have a curiosity about individual stocks and want to try your luck, go for it. But don't use more than 10% of your portfolio on such adventures." This was news to me and an exciting concept, to say the least. In the end, the stock market is fun to watch, and it almost feels a little like gambling. So, I decided to put 5% of my portfolio into a company I really enjoy and think is a prospering and emerging company.

Again, I am not here to give you stock-picking advice. Instead, I am here to tell you that it is OK to indulge your curiosity and invest in individual stocks that interest you, so long as it does not take over most of your portfolio. As a general rule of thumb, no more than 10% of your portfolio should be invested in individual stocks or any other investment that might interest you. The additional 90% should be invested in a safer venture, like index funds. The 90/10 principle is a mere guideline and not a rule. Nevertheless, you should know why you invest in individual stocks and what you would like to get out of them. I wish I could go back to Adam and ask him these questions:

- Why are you investing in Bitcoin?
- How much of your portfolio are you devoting to this hot trend?
- How does Bitcoin price move?
- When will you pull out?
- What are you looking to get out of Bitcoin?
- What could cause Bitcoin to crash?

- Are you only investing in Bitcoin because everyone else is?
- Who is the founder of Bitcoin? (Because no one seems to know.)

So many people have failed to think critically about why they invested in their chosen stocks. My brother did not ask himself enough legitimate questions about whether the financial decisions he was making were wise ones. Bobby taught me that if you want to be 100% invested in index funds, that is perfectly fine. And if you're going to dabble in picking individual stocks, that is OK too. If that is the case, it is critical to know why you choose not to make a surer investment in index funds. You will be missing out on the index's superior returns to gamble on actively investing returns.

It is also important to note that you have moved back into active investing when you start investing in individual stocks, and you will need to pay someone to execute those trades. It is true that, had you bought Apple when it first started, you would be a millionaire now. However, if people who devote their lives to analyze financial data cannot do it with any remarkable degree of accuracy, what makes you think you can? Before you invest in an individual stock, ask yourself the same questions I wish I asked my brother.

- Why are you investing in X?
- How much of your portfolio are you devoting to this endeavor?
- How does X price move? What influences it?
- When will you pull out? Is this a short- or long-term project?
- What are you looking to get out of X?
- What could cause X to crash?
- Are you only investing in X because everyone else is?

If you do not have definite answers to 75% of these questions, you need to seriously consider if investing in this stock or hot trend is a good idea. Do not get caught up in the new trends, financial fads, and get-rich-quick schemes. The premise of this book is to give you the education to make more educated decisions in investing. If you cannot back up with evidence your decision to invest in the hot new trend or a company's stock, then there should be no reason to do it. I am not saying the evidence is not possible. I am only telling you you need to seek it out and comprehend it.

Chapter 12
Rebalancing

Core Principle:
Halftime adjustments win games.

Adam and I are huge football fans. We are from Buffalo, where everyone is a Buffalo Bills fan. Yes, the ones who jump through tables. Except, we do not jump through tables, and my brother, for some reason, is a New England Patriots fan.

Nevertheless, one of the most critical skills a team can have is knowing how to make adjustments during the game. If running the ball hasn't worked during the first half, a good team will note that and begin to pass the ball more during the second half. Adjusting their strategy throughout a game helps teams win. Similarly, you need to make adjustments to keep your portfolio on track to help you succeed financially.

This chapter will cover rebalancing your portfolio, the process of buying and/or selling some of your portfolio when your asset allocation is skewed. What does that mean?

Let us say that your investment goals have recently changed, or maybe you have recently become more or less risk-averse. You can buy or sell parts of your portfolio to better reflect your new goals, feelings about risk, or time horizon. Alternatively, maybe one of your investments has done very well recently and has increased in value. It is now a more significant portion of your portfolio, and perhaps you do not want that investment to make up that much of your finances.

It is vital to rebalance because it helps you return your allocation to what you want it to be, or it can help you move into a new allocation as time goes on. This is a critical concept to understand because your chosen allocation has a corresponding risk level. When you change your allocation, it will likely lead to a new risk level, and new risk levels bring further consequences. Remember, you chose a particular allocation for the "consequences" it would produce. You carefully selected what your portfolio comprises based on what financial goals you have. Although there is no perfect time to rebalance, failing to do so when necessary can lead to your finances getting off track of helping you meet your investing goals.

This chapter will describe how an allocation becomes unbalanced and why it is important to check your account and rebalance periodically.

Adam asked me how his allocation could become skewed in the first place. I gave him this example: Let us suppose I invest $50 in stocks and $50 in bonds, which is my entire portfolio. My allocation is 50% stocks and 50% bonds. In a given year, my stocks do well, and they are now worth $60. My bonds do poorly, and they are now worth $40. My allocation is now 60% stocks and 40% bonds. Obviously, this is greatly simplified, but you can see how an ever-changing financial market changes your portfolio's makeup.

This seemed to worry Adam. He was concerned that his allocation would change too much and how he could keep this from happening. There is no way to maintain your exact desired percentages at all times. Your portfolio will fluctuate around your allocation. There will come a time when you have to rebalance it and bring it back to where you want it to be.

Your allocation will periodically become skewed. You can be confident of this because some funds will do better than others, which will change your portfolio's composition. You can find these percentages on the website where you trade. If these percentages fluctuate between +/-5%, there is no need for immediate rebalancing unless you want to. When your allocation is more than 10 to 15% off for multiple weeks, that means some funds are doing way better than others. Now, 10 to 15% is not exact math or science; it may be 20 to 30% for you if you are comfortable with the fluctuating risk. This means it may be time to sell off the funds that are doing well and buy some more of the dipping funds. This, of course, is the crucial rule of investing: Buy low and sell high. This will prove massively beneficial for you in the end.

Remember that you do not need to check every day if your allocation is off by 10% or more. Doing so periodically will be just fine. Rebalancing is not an activity that you must do every year on the dot. You could possibly go multiple years without having to rebalance.

If you want to rebalance, you should ask yourself some questions. What will selling off shares in a particular account do? What sort of taxes and costs will I pay if I rebalance? These questions are essential to someone who chooses to rebalance more than once a year. There is a lot of financial jargon associated with selling mutual funds. I will not bore you with it, but let us go over the key concepts.

First, it is crucial to note which account you are selling shares are in. Due to their nature, different accounts will have other implications on the taxes you pay. For example, you have already paid taxes on the money you put into Roth IRA but not the money you put into a Traditional IRA.

Secondly, you need to know that you can minimize the capital gains taxes you will pay by selling funds after you have owned them for more than a year. At that point, you will typically be taxed around 15%. Selling funds in a taxable account that you have held for less than a year will create capital gains to be taxed as ordinary income, which is taxed according to your personal tax bracket. Another way to rebalance to minimize taxes and costs is simply to invest more heavily in underperforming funds. This will raise its dropping allocation without having to sell anything, which would have adverse tax effects. I am not a CPA and am no expert on tax advice, but I have learned that if you think selling your funds may cause adverse tax effects for you, talking to a tax professional may be worth its weight in gold.

If all of this seems too complicated and annoying, firms sell funds that will rebalance themselves. However, they do come at a slightly higher expense for this reason. Rebalancing is a natural and vital part of investing. It does not take more than looking at your percentages a couple times a year and making sure your risk level is stable.

The main goal of this book is to be easily understood by all sorts of investors. When I showed Adam the next topic, he balked at all the math. But I'll try not to make this tedious or complicated. First, let us talk about something called reversion to the mean. Then, we will talk through the steps you can take to rebalance. The math is NOT hard. All you need is a calculator for the example.

In a paper called "Mean reversion in stock prices: Evidence and Implications" by James Poterba and Lawrence Summers,[10] they hypothesize that stock prices will tend to revert towards their average price over time. I would not recommend this paper to the average reader. Instead, I will summarize and tell you that the article looks to confirm that the stock market is not a random walk. Over time, the prices of stock will typically move towards what it has historically averaged. This paper, which has been cited close to 3,500 times, could not consistently reject the hypothesis that the stock market follows a random walk. They did find some serial correlation in stock returns over both short and long periods, which further indicates that the stock market may not be truly random.

This is important because if you believe that stocks revert to their mean price over time, this will incentivize a rebalance by selling high and buying low. When you sell high, you sell some

10 Poterba, J., & Summers, L. (1987). Mean reversion in stock prices: evidence and implications. https://doi.org/10.3386/w2343

winners. Those winners will eventually revert down to their mean. When you buy stocks that are priced low, you can then watch those prices revert up to the mean. This hypothesis would mean a win-win for investors who rebalance. This might seem boring, but this phenomenon is fascinating to economists. At the very least, it is vital to grasp the basic premise.

Next, let us run through an example of how to rebalance. I will illustrate how the math is done to rebalance your portfolio. I vastly over-simplify the model because there may be more than one fund for stocks or bonds. Nevertheless, the math is simple and can easily be translated for personal use. Please see the Appendix for a more in-depth version of this example; there, I run through where all the numbers are exactly coming from:

Asset	Initial Investment	Portion of Portfolio	Year 1 Return	Year 1 Amount in the Account	Portion of Portfolio
Stocks	$500	62.50%	49%	$745	74.06%
Bonds	$300	37.50%	-13%	$261	25.94%
Total	$800	100%		$1,006	100%

We now see that our allocation is off by more than 10 to 15% for both our bond and stock portions of our allocation. We can handle this in two ways: First, we could sell off some of our stocks and buy more bonds.

Asset	Year 1 Amount in the Account	Portion of Portfolio	Buy and Sell	The New Portion in the Account
Stocks	$745	74.06%	Sell $116.26 of the stocks	62.50%
Bonds	$261	25.94%	Buy $116.26 worth of bonds	37.50%
Total	$1,006	100%	$1,006	100%

The second way to handle this is to only buy the asset that is dipping in percentage.

Asset	Year 1 Amount in the Account	Portion of Portfolio	Buy and Sell	The New Portion in The Account
Stocks	$745	74.06%	Do nothing	62.50%
Bonds	$261	25.94%	Buy $186 worth of bonds	37.50%
Total	$1,006	100%	$1,192	100%

Here are a couple quick tips when thinking about rebalancing:

1. Some funds can rebalance your portfolio for you. You put in your desired allocation and an interval of where it is allowed to fluctuate. If all of this seems complicated or like too much work, those types of funds may be beneficial. You can pay slightly more to not have to worry about rebalancing.
2. Rebalancing your tax-deferred or brokerage accounts may have different tax ramifications. Some accounts may allow you to rebalance without any tax implications.

3. If you do not like your allocation or choice of individual funds, rebalancing can be a wise time to move to a new desired allocation or to sell off funds that you no longer want in your portfolio: two birds, one stone.
4. When you start withdrawing funds from your accounts, you can also take that as an opportunity to rebalance. Again, you will be accomplishing two things at once.
5. Be aware of what time of the year you choose to rebalance. This can have implications on how you will be taxed. Selecting to rebalance at one point in the year over another can allow you to place your finances under different tax bills.
6. For the most part, broad index funds will do some rebalancing on their own.

Again, this chapter is merely the guidelines on when and how to rebalance. The truth is that rebalancing is dependent on your personal risks and goals. Rebalancing is necessary and important when trying to reach long-term goals. This is important because as time passes, risks and objectives will inevitably change too. For example, when you are 35 and just starting to save for retirement, you can have a riskier portfolio that is very stock orientated because you have a lot of time to deal with those bad and good years that stocks give you. However, as you move closer to retirement age, you need to start trading in those stocks for more bonds to reduce year-to-year fluctuation in your account.

Chapter 13

Retirement by the Pool

Core Principle:

Retirement planning is like working out to be in shape for the summer. If you start early, there is a great chance you would have a six-pack by the summer. If you start thinking about retirement while you are young, there is a good chance you will retire comfortably.

It was a hot summer, especially for Buffalo; I had finally made it home from my second year at Alabama. My dad, Adam, and I were out by the pool in our backyard celebrating my brother finally graduating and accepting a prestigious job with a tremendous medical firm. We enjoyed the cool water when my dad started asking about the retirement options Adam had been given at the firm. Adam was perplexed, but he knew they had some sort of 401(k) match. While in the pool, I slowly talked him through the intricacies of retirement investing.

This chapter will be brief, but I hope it will give you a starting point for different vehicles for saving for retirement. I am going to cover the basics of 401(k), IRA, and Roth IRAs. All have their unique pros and cons. Therefore, picking what works best for your life and portfolio may take some research of your own.

401(k)

The first vehicle we will look at is one that almost everyone has heard of: a 401(k). A 401(k) is a retirement plan offered through your place of employment. Not all 401(k)s are created equal. I repeat: All 401(k)s are not created equal. Your 401(k) is limited by the company that employs you. Depending on the tax and financial priorities of your employer, your 401(k) can be structured differently.

Many people, like my brother, do not thoroughly research or fully look into the 401(k) options offered by their employer. This is a dangerous game to play. Your employer might select a 401(k) firm that has your best financial interest at heart. Alternatively, they could choose one that minimizes the firm's cost. If this is the case, then your 401(k) might only offer you the option to select between multiple actively managed funds to invest in. If you do not do your research, you could be none the wiser about the financial opportunities you are missing by being forced into investing in actively managed portfolios. Therefore, it may be of interest to you to determine precisely how your 401(k) is structured, how much your match is, and the available investment vehicles. Let's list some pros and cons and see if it makes sense for you to contribute.

Pros

- 401(k) contributions are automatically deducted from your pay, which leads to an out-of-sight, out-of-mind benefit.
- Contributions can reduce taxable income.
- Everyone can hold other retirement accounts outside of their 401(k).
- Most companies offer a contribution match, i.e., free money to invest. A match means if you put in 3% of your salary, your company will match your 3% and help you save a total of 6%. Most companies that have a match will have a cap on the match.
- These assets can be carried or rolled over from employer to employer.

- Contributions and capital gains are not taxed until distribution.
- The contribution limit in 2020 is $19,500 for those under 50 and $26,000 for those over 50.[11]

Cons

- Investments can be run by actively managed funds, draining the return of precious little two percentages.
- Some companies have no contribution match.
- Depending on your employer's investment company choice, there can be a limited variety of investment options.
- You are not able to access your contributions until 59 and a half without penalty for early withdrawal.

I know what you are thinking: "Zack will advise against a 401(k) because he mentioned the possibility of actively managed portfolios." Typically, I would avoid actively managed funds, but a contribution match is like free money to invest. Other vehicles limit the amount of your annual contribution.

With that being said, if your employer offers a match, I would recommend your first savings for retirement should be the amount required to receive the company match. Then, you can take the remaining money you want to save for retirement and look at vehicles like an IRA or Roth IRA. My brother said he would look into his company's 401(k) more closely and get the match. His next question was, "What is the difference between a Roth and Traditional IRA?"

Traditional IRA

A Traditional IRA is another vehicle that allows investors to contribute for retirement, with some tax advantages and other facets 401(k)s might not be able to offer. Let us look at some pros and cons of investing a portion of your retirement savings into a Traditional IRA.

---

11 https://www.irs.gov/retirement-plans/plan-participant-employee/retirement-topics-401k-and-profit-sharing-plan-contribution-limits

Pros

- All contributed money is tax-deferred, which means that you only pay taxes when the money is taken out of the account.
- There are potentially more options than 401(k)s for things to invest in, depending on your employer.
- IRA can provide the investor tax deductions.

Cons

- There are strict limits to what one can contribute to a Traditional IRA. That limit is $6,000 for those under 50, and $7,000 for those older than 50, as of 2020.[12]
- You are not able to access the funds until the age of 59 and a half without penalty.
- Required withdrawals from IRA start at 70 and a half.

Roth IRA

A Roth IRA is another vehicle similar to a Traditional IRA with different tax implications. Let's look at the pros and cons

Pros

- With a Roth IRA, money is taxed on the way into the account and tax-free when coming out of the account.
- Traditional IRAs require withdrawals at 70 and a half. A Roth IRA never requires withdrawals, which means it can be passed to the next generation if desired.
- There are potentially more options than 401(k)s for things to invest in, depending on your employer.

Cons

- There are no tax deductions since one is paying taxes when they make contributions.
- There are strict limits to what one can contribute to a Roth

12 *Retirement topics - 401(k) and profit-sharing plan contribution limits*. Internal Revenue Service. (n.d.). https://www.irs.gov/retirement-plans/plan-participant-employee/retirement-topics-401k-and-profit-sharing-plan-contribution-limits

IRA. That limit is $6,000 for those under 50, and $7,000 for those older than 50, as of 2020.[13]
- You are not able to access the funds until the age of 59 and a half without penalty.
- There are income limits on who can contribute. For single investors, you need to make less than $122,000, and for joint investors (investing with a spouse), you need to make less than a combined total of $193,000.

Summary

As you can see, each of these investment vehicles offers different advantages and has other drawbacks. First, you should take whatever match an employer gives you. Then look to invest in a Roth or a Traditional IRA.

The biggest question when determining whether one should use a Roth or Traditional IRA is all about tax rates. If you believe that your tax rate will be higher in retirement, then choose a Roth to take advantage of contributions that are taxed at a lower rate now. If you believe your tax rate will be lower in retirement, then choose a Traditional IRA to defer taxes to a period when your tax rate will be lower. If you are interested in learning more about Roth and Traditional IRAs, CPAs (certified public accountant) can provide more advice on properly handling this decision based on your unique tax bracket. There are even ways to start with a Traditional IRA and later move to a Roth. Also, you can have multiple IRA accounts, but your contribution to all of them combined must not exceed the contribution limits. In other words, the summed total one can contribute to both a Roth and Traditional IRA is $6,000 for those under 50 and $7,000 for those over 50. One can only contribute X amount to a Roth IRA and "contribution limit minus X" to a Traditional IRA in any given year. Therefore, if you are under 50 and put all $6,000 in a

13 *Retirement topics - 401(k) and profit-sharing plan contribution limits*. Internal Revenue Service. (n.d.). https://www.irs.gov/retirement-plans/plan-participant-employee/retirement-topics-401k-and-profit-sharing-plan-contribution-limits

Traditional IRA, you are not legally allowed to put in any money in a Roth IRA that year.

Retirement may seem far off for you. But remember, starting early will allow compounding interest to work its wonders. If you can only start with 1% of your yearly salary, DO IT! Your future self will thank you.

Note that 401(k)s are set up through your employer, while Roth and Traditional IRAs are set up individually and separately from your employment.

Next, we will discuss how to start distributing funds from your accounts. This is an essential step. You have done the hard part to invest the money. The worst thing you can do is over-spend, over-use the account, and drain it too quickly.

Factors that Erode Returns

One last thing before we get to the topic of distribution of funds is something even more critical: the erosion of funds. My brother said, "If I have $2 million in my Roth IRA by the time I retire, then I will not have to worry about a single thing!" That got me thinking about what factors we always need to be conscious of, even when we are invested in a Roth IRA.

1. Behavior
2. Taxes
3. Fees
4. Inflation

First and foremost, your behavior. Your behavior is most important because if you cannot invest properly and with the right mindset, taxes, fees, and inflation won't even matter.

Second, taxes are everywhere. If your Roth IRA is not being taxed, then something else is. Always factor in taxes and how much they are going to diminish your purchasing power. As Benjamin Franklin famously said, "Nothing is certain but death and taxes."

Next is fees. We have discussed costs extensively in this book, so at this point, you should be aware of how detrimental a 2%

service fee can be on your returns. Always remember: They take percentages instead of dollars because most people are bad at statistics! (Kidding. Mostly. No one would use an advisor if they saw how much that 2% really cost them in dollar-converted returns over their lifetime.)

Last but not least, inflation. You can think of inflation as a negative return on your money. Inflation has historically been 2 to 3%; in other words, you lose close to 2 to 3% of your purchasing power each year. You typically want to stay ahead of inflation; if you return 2% this year and inflation is 3%, you really lost 1% in purchasing power.

Chapter 14

Distribution of Funds

Core Principle:
Live below your means.

I hope that when reading this section, you will get a sense of the necessary details to keep in mind after you have amassed a large sum of money in each of your accounts. All that needs to be done now is to figure out how to distribute that money from your account for you to use.

My brother asked, "When I get that $2 million in my retirement account, how do I use it efficiently so I will not run out of money?" I told him that was a long way off, but the short answer is to live below your means.

Then he asked, "If I set up a brokerage account for buying my first house, do I pull all my money out and pay in cash?" To answer that question, we looked at IRA, Roth IRA, and regular brokerage accounts and how that money will be taxed.

IRA

In a Traditional IRA account, you are deferring taxes until you start withdrawing. Therefore, once you start withdrawing, you will begin paying ordinary income taxes on whatever is removed from the account.

Roth IRA

The beauty of the Roth IRA is you already paid taxes when you invested in it. So, whatever you withdraw after age 59 and a half is not taxed. If you amassed $2.5 million, all of that $2.5 million is yours, and none is Uncle Sam's at that point.

Brokerage Account

Calculating taxes on mutual funds is a bit more complicated. Depending on the fund sold, you could be taxed at your ordinary tax rate, a long-term tax rate, or possibly even not at all.

Again, I cannot stress enough the importance of tiny percentages. So, hiring a CPA to help minimize taxes through your account's distributions can be incredibly valuable. The most important concept to grasp in the distribution phase is the significance of not using your money up.

So, let us start to unpack that. Remember that you want to begin to minimize risk and fluctuation in your accounts when you get closer and closer to retirement or withdrawal periods. This essentially means investing in safer investments, like bonds. This is important because stocks can fluctuate wildly between years. You do not want that uncertainty when it comes time to take your money out. Bonds can still lose value, but there is less fluctuation between years. This is why the strategy of carrying your age in bonds has made sense for so many people.

So, why's this important?

To understand the importance of risk associated with fluctuating stocks and bonds, we need to know how volatile they are. In other words, how much they move. Try to stay with me here because you might get some unwanted flashbacks from high school math. We need to understand the standard deviation to comprehend the volatility of stocks and bonds.

For example, let us say that stock returns have a standard deviation of 15%, and bond returns have a standard deviation of 5%. If we believe that stock and bond returns are normally distributed, we can make the following claims:

15% ◄◄◄ Stocks ►►► -15%
5% ◄ Bonds ► -5%

We can expect that around 68% of the daily returns will be between one standard deviation in an average year. In other words, 68% of daily returns will be between 15 and -15% for stocks, and 68% of daily returns will be between 5 and -5% for bonds. Let us go even further to illustrate this point.

30% ◄◄◄◄◄◄ Stocks ►►►►►► -30%
10% ◄◄ Bonds ►► -10%

Given help from normally distributed properties, we can expect that around 95% of the daily returns will be between two standard deviations in an average year. In other words, 95% of daily returns will be between 30 and -30% for stocks, and 95% of daily returns will be between 10 and -10% for bonds. From the graph above, you can see that bonds typically give an investor less return over time and less standard deviation/volatility. In other words, bonds are, on average, a safer investment but also less profitable.

In the graph above, the standard deviation is used as a tool to measure volatility. Bonds have a smaller deviation, which leads to less return. However, when distributing funds, minimizing volatility is essential. Let us look at an example of why that is so critical.

Why is it important? Because math sometimes does not work how you would like it to. If Jim loses 30% from his $2 million retirement account, how much of a return does he need to get back to the $2 million mark? Are you thinking 30%? Try close to 43%! Let's do the math:

Loss of 30%:	►	$2,000,000 * 0.7 = $1,400,000
Gain of 30%:	►	$1,400,000 * 1.3 = $1,820,000
Gain of 42.85%:	►	$1,400,000 * 1.4285 = $2,000,000

In retirement, we no longer have time on our side. After distributing a percentage of our account each year, we want to see a number in our account close to that original number next year. The principal should stay constant over time. If you are still heavily invested in stocks in retirement, one bad year could deplete a large portion of the nest egg you spent years to achieve. When you are no longer contributing and are slowly draining the account in retirement, losing a considerable amount can destroy how much you can withdraw each year. It can have devastating financial effects. To minimize this risk, it may be wise to reinvest any withdrawals you did not use in the early years of your retirement. This will help maintain a constant principal in your account that will allow you to take out the desired percentage year after year. This will enable you to keep your lifestyle for the duration of your retirement.

Live Below Your Means

Suppose someone had a bond index that yields 5% annually. She has $2 million in her retirement account, and she could live off a 4% withdrawal from that account each year. That would be $80,000 every year. This person's account would stay very close to that $2 million threshold after each year's end.

Being smart and living below your average return can help increase your chances of never outliving your money and decrease your chances of having to go back to work!

Here is what to keep in mind when distributing funds:

1. Which account are you drawing from? This will determine tax implications.
2. How are you going to drain your account? A yearly percentage, total withdrawal, or larger periodic withdrawals? This can often be answered by referencing the primary purpose of the account. Let us say you opened an account to buy a house: When you have the money in the account, you do not necessarily need to immediately drain all of it to pay off the house. It could be more financially advantageous to take percentages out of that account each year to pay off a mortgage that is 3% each year. You could continue to make money that way! If you can return more than the mortgage costs each year, you can pay the interest and have nearly free

money left over to reinvest or spend. Amassing money is the hard part. Once you have it, you can use that account value to your advantage. There could potentially be extenuating circumstances that would require you to pull all the money from your account. However, you should know how you can make an account work for you before you drain your account completely.

3. How is your allocation looking now that you have entered a distribution phase?
4. Living below your means and reinvesting extra income can help keep your account at the desired level.

Here is a little story for those that may never even see $80,000 a year when working: There was once a man named Steve. Steve was a janitor for a public school in Texas. Steve made $23,000 a year. He was smart, though. He saved and invested close to 40% of his salary in index funds. At an interest rate of 10%, when he retired 40 years later, he had amassed close to $5 million! Now, if he took 4% out a year when he retired, he would be living off of $200,000 a year. Keep that in mind when thinking about your future.

Distribution is the easy part of the whole investing process because you now get to spend the money you have been saving for years. Remember that being competent at the beginning of a distribution phase can help you in later years of the distribution phase. Moreover, if you ever want $2 million in your retirement account, you will need to sacrifice extra percentages each month to get there. This may mean giving up one coffee a week or eating out one less day a week. Find the money to make those sacrifices. Your future self will thank you when you will receive $80,000 a year in retirement.

But now it's time to start implementing the plan! We will assume that by now you have an account set up with some large and reputable firms like Schwab, Fidelity, Vanguard, etc. Let us get to the actual buttons you need to start pressing to implement your plan.

Chapter 15
Website Guide and Plan

Core Principle:
Action is the mechanism that propels us.

If you are like me, sometimes you can understand all the details and tools you need to succeed, but sometimes you are overwhelmed by a new process—like actually setting up your accounts. Therefore, my goal in this chapter is to help guide you through the actual button-pushing steps required to start investing in index funds. I do not want you to be paralyzed by fear.

First, visit the investing website of your choice; we have discussed your options earlier in the book. I will generically illustrate the steps, but most websites will be somewhat similar. This is a relatively painless and straightforward process, but it may look complicated and daunting if you have never done it before.

By now, you and my brother can start implementing the information I have presented in this book. I aim to make this chapter detailed and straightforward enough that it would be easy for Adam to follow along when he is ready to start investing.

Step 1

If you have not done so already, set up which account you would like: brokerage, Roth IRA and/or Traditional IRA, etc. If you have not, start choosing which account you would like to set up first and follow the website's directions to set it up. You will most likely have to give some personal information and need to connect your bank account. They will ask for very private information, so it is imperative to pick a large and reputable firm. It may take a few days to link your bank account. Come back after that is completed.

Step 2

Once you have set up an account of your choice, you might want to set up another account. You can pick an additional account you'd like to set up at the top sections of most websites. If you have trouble finding the specific tab for your website, I suggest calling your firm or using Google. First, let us deal with one account. Once you know the steps to set up one, you can set up multiple.

Step 3

After you have created an account, you will see that account has $0 in the cash column and $0 in a balance or value column. Your cash column is money you have transferred from a bank or institution to your chosen account. This money is not invested yet, but simply cash ready to be invested. Your balance or value column is money that is invested in that chosen account.

Step 4

Next, we want to transfer money from our bank account or other financial institution to your designated account. You can do this by going to the transfer page, which should be in one of the top sections, and choosing an account, like your bank account, to take funds from and put that money into one of the accounts you set up. When you are doing this, you will find that most firms allow an investor to set up a recurring transfer. This is not automatically invested for you. Instead, it will automatically take money from your bank account each designated period and put it in your cash column for you to invest.

Step 5

After a day or two, when you see that money has successfully been transferred and is in your cash column, then it is time to designate a place you will invest in. Again, your cash column is typically located on the home page. Remember not to invest without money in your cash column.

Step 6

Once you have the cash to use in your account, you will want to go to the trade tab. Under the trade tab, find trade funds/trade mutual funds.

Step 7

At the top, you can pick and choose which account you are using for the trade. Be careful you are clicked onto the correct account before you trade.

Step 8

Next, you will want to do a little research. Most firms offer an excellent way of viewing most stocks, bonds, mutual funds, and such they offer. You can find funds to invest in using the search tool on your firms' websites. I will name a few funds that may be of interest to you and how they may correspond to your allocations.

Fund	Details	Stock Allocation	Bond Allocation
SWAGX FXNAX VBTLX	Tracks the performance of the Bloomberg Barclays US Aggregate Bond Index – Schwab/Fidelity/Vanguard Funds, respectively		X
SWTSX SWPPX	Tracks the performance of the US stock market following the Dow Jones/ S&P 500 – Schwab Funds	X	
SWISX FSPSX	Tracks the performance of non-US companies – Schwab/Fidelity Fund, respectively	X	

Your options are not limited to these funds. Please do some research of your own, looking at the information the website provides on these funds.

There are many funds to choose from. They do not need to be funds that are only "Schwab Funds" or "Fidelity Funds." If the details look suitable to your financial goals and offer no-load, no-fee, and the operating expenses are low, they should be OK for your portfolio.

Be careful to look through the website's information on each fund. They will give detailed breakdowns of each fund. Note that you can buy "Fidelity Funds" on the Schwab website and vice versa. Schwab does not only sell Schwab funds; they have hundreds of different options.

The great part about this process is that you can make it as simple or complex as you like. You could select just one stock index and one bond index as your desired allocation. Alternatively, you could choose a great many.

Simply by going to the search bar and searching for a fund name, you can find out so much about it. The information there can help you verify that the expense ratios are low and a no-load (fee) to buy or sell shares. You can investigate the risk of the fund as well as how it has historically performed. The rating of the fund is typically listed as well. This information found on the brokerage house websites is compelling, and you must use it to your advantage.

Step 9

Once you know which funds you would like to invest in, you want to break up the money you have available to determine percentages. I am going to go through a simple example and how the math works. Say for your brokerage account you have $100 to invest per month, and you want to invest 33% in the bond index, 33% in the US stock index, and 34% in the international index. For each fund, you would click the trade and buy buttons and spend $33 to purchase whichever bond index you would like, $33 to purchase whichever US index you'd like, and $34 to purchase whichever international index you'd like.

In summary, the necessary steps are to make sure you are on the correct account you want to use, click "trade" or "trade mutual funds" on the ticker you would like to buy—for example, "SWRSX"—and click "buy." It will prompt an amount, you enter what you'd like to allocate in dollars, and click "confirm." If you have trouble with percentages, Google offers fantastic calculators.

Mutual funds will not be confirmed until the end of the business day. Therefore, you will not see your orders enacted until that night or the next day.

Step 10

The brokerage websites will typically ask if you would like to reinvest dividends and capital gains. When you are in the compounding phase, reinvesting those dividends and capital gains is crucial.

Step 11

Once you have finished all that, you will want to do the same for any other accounts you might have. You might want to set up automatic investing if you meet the minimum requirements. If that is the case, you will have to set up automatic withdrawals from your bank account each month (or some other given period of your choice) for the automatic investing to work. Automatic investing is the easiest option, but it typically requires a minimum investment per fund each time you would like to invest. When I first started investing, I could not use this option, and that is OK. However, you will want to set up automatic withdrawals from your bank into one or all of your accounts. Then you will need to manually do step 10 each investment period.

Do not be afraid to just play around with the website of your brokerage house. Familiarize yourself with its interface and the different tools it offers. Do not freak out trying to find the best funds to invest in. The key is to start investing as soon as possible with funds and allocations you feel comfortable with.

This was one of the most daunting parts of the process for me, personally. It can be so hard, but I told myself it was crucial to sit down and do something in this step! Action is sometimes scary and challenging, but in the end, no activity in itself is an action. Remember that. One of my favorite quotes is attributed to Tony Robbins: "You see, in life, lots of people know what to do, but few people actually do what they know. Knowing is not enough! You must take action."

One thing I purposely left out of this chapter is information on ETFs. ETFs, or exchange-traded funds, are a type of security said to combine the benefits of mutual funds, stocks, and bonds, but which can be traded throughout the day. I left that out of the book because I am trying to promote long-term investing principles and advice, and it seems ETFs are more geared towards day-to-day trading and not the year-to-year trading I am preaching.

Chapter 16
Brain Train

Core Principle:
Everyone can get to the gym when they are feeling great. It is those days when you are tired and drained that you need to get to the gym most. Because the latter days will far outnumber the former days.

You have made it! You are now a more diverse, educated, and well-rounded investor. This is something to be celebrated! Most people think ignorance is bliss, but if ignorance means I could lose hundreds of thousands of my own dollars, I'd much rather be aware and educated. You are now more educated yourself. If you found this topic interesting and want to read more, I would recommend books like *Unshakeable* and *Money: Master the Game* by Tony Robbins, as well as *The Bogleheads' Guide* by Lindauer, Larimore, and LeBoeuf.

In this chapter, I want to stress to you once again the importance of remaining invested. My brother and many other new investors are tempted to enter and exit the market as it fluctuates. I cannot advise strongly enough against this. If a crashing market scares you or a correction would cause you to make radical alterations to your portfolio, put a Post-it on this chapter for pleasure reading.

Even if you do not see yourself as the kind of investor that would make that sort of decision when the stock market seems to be doing a nosedive or after talking to an ignorant friend/colleague, reread this chapter. I mean it. Make a note and come back to this chapter. It will continue to be essential for years to come.

You will need to read this chapter more than once. Getting started is hard, but the hard part is not over. It has only begun. You are dealing with real money. Your hard-earned money! You may lose 30% and gain 60% or vice versa. That uncertainty is scary! To quell that fear, it is crucial to consider your loss or gain within the larger perspective that the stock market has consistently trended upwards.

If you cannot deal with the fear of a market downturn and choose to pull your money from the market, your investment ventures will not be as successful. That sounds harsh. However, if you do not believe in the effects of compound interest or the stock market's upward trend, your portfolio will suffer. This is true regardless of what sort of allocation you have.

Here is the good news: You know the facts. You know the statistics. You see the trend. You know why you are investing. You know what you are investing in. You understand the power of indexing. You comprehend the power of compounding. With these facts, you should have the confidence to proceed! However, let us go through some thoughts and questions that may arise when times are tough.

Thought

If I pull my money out, I will put it back in when the market bottoms out.

Response

Can you tell the future? No. First, it is nearly impossible to time the market consistently. Second, pulling your money out can lead to taxes and unexpected capital gains costs. If you can tell when the market will bottom out and time the market, you will not require index funds! Remember, if you had missed just the top 50 days for the S&P 500 index returns over its lifetime, you would yield 14.4 times less money than if you just stayed invested. That is a damn close window to be flirting with.

Thought

My neighbor John told me index funds are only for very risk-averse people. He said they will not yield me the superior returns he has had in the past few years.

Response

Ask John for his average returns minus advisor fees over the lifetime of his investing. If it is anywhere near 10%, you might want to consider talking to his advisor. However, if it is around 5 to 7% and is losing money in fees to invest on top of that, he could lose thousands of dollars throughout his investing career. I would recommend to your neighbor John that he look closely at the numbers.

Thought

Everyone is saying we are in for a bear market. Let me pull my money out early and wait until it is over.

Response

See the answer to the first thought. You cannot tell the future. You cannot time the market. Oh, and by the way, no one else can consistently do so either.

Thought

An advisor said she returned over 40% last year for her clients. That is quadruple the average return for index funds. Should I invest with her?

Response

Ask for her average return minus fees over the last five, 10, and 20 years. She may be a lot more apprehensive about giving those numbers to you. All advisors are not created equal, so if you choose to go down that road, be conscious of what you are signing up for and how much it will cost you.

Thought

This guy on television who graduated from Harvard with six degrees advises everyone to invest in [insert gimmicky stock advice] (e.g., penny stocks, etc.). He says that it is the next Apple.

Response

Can he tell the future? No. If someone knew which company would be the next Apple, would they parade around telling people for a small salary when they could make so much more by entirely investing in that stock? Do not get caught up in people's titles or unwarranted advice.

Note: Many well-known investors have invested in the stock market with extraordinarily high efficiency. Names like Warren Buffet, Carl Icahn, and George Soros come to mind. Do me a favor and Google "Warren Buffet's advice on index funds." Warren Buffet, the billionaire investor, advocates that most ordinary people should invest in index funds rather than try their hand at stock picking. "My regular recommendation has been a low-cost S&P 500 index fund," Buffett wrote in his 2016 Berkshire Hathaway annual shareholder letter.[14] Should you listen to that Harvard guy or listen to billionaire investor Warren Buffet?

Thought

Why isn't everyone investing in index funds?

Response

One thing you need to know about the financial advising market is that it is incredibly lucrative. The industry spends hundreds of millions of dollars a year advertising to get people to think

14 Shareholder letters. (n.d.). www.berkshirehathaway.com/letters/letters.html

they are geniuses and can handle all your finances for you. Marketing is a very persuasive technique; even if you know the truth and believe it will not influence you. On the other hand, maybe people do not want to take the time to educate themselves on the topic.

Thought

I am too scared to do it.

Response

Not making a decision *is* a decision. Those that choose to not invest in anything and merely save their money will have their purchasing power diminished on average 3% each year. This is caused by inflation. For you to do anything of value, you must jump, leap, or step forward, or else you'll be trapped in stagnation. If you are still confused about the steps you need to take to proceed, find someone who understands the principles we've discussed in this book that can help you implement index investing.

Thought

No one in my family has ever invested in the stock market, bond market, or anything else.

Response

Why do you think most people refrain from investing in the stock market? They are uneducated, do not know how to invest, or do not trust the stock market. Distrust in the financial services market typically stems from a lack of education. However, you are now educated and understand the process. You know the fees, trends, and numbers. You have the knowledge required to be the first person in your family to make the intelligent decision to take advantage of index funds. If you want further information, I would suggest reading a longer, more detail-oriented book like *Money: Master the Game* by Tony Robbins.

Thought

I do not have enough money to invest right now.

Response

Bullshit! Schwab offers a $1 minimum per fund. Only 1$! Can't you save $1? It is OK to start small. Remember the power of compounding? If you invest $1 a month for 40 years at a return of 10%, you could expect to earn close to $6,000! And you only invested a total of $480! You only invest $12 a year. This is obviously a dramatic simplification, but the truth is you can start investing with "pennies" of your yearly earnings.

Thought

The stock market is too volatile! Up 25% this year, down 41% next year. I cannot handle that.

Response

In investing, volatility in returns is guaranteed. You cannot get around that fact. If you understand the stock market is necessarily volatile and you cannot sit on the sideline, you must find a way to cope with the volatility. There are various solutions to this that range from having an allocation primarily composed of bonds to not allowing yourself to look at your account numbers during downturns. Volatility is like the common cold: we know it will happen once or twice a year, and there is nothing we can do about it. It is part of life. If you stay inside and hide from the cold, you will miss the best aspects of life. If you sit on the sidelines and fear volatility, you will miss the best returns available.

Thought

I studied [insert savvy major]. I should know this.

Response

I have been institutionally educated on mathematics, economics, and finance. It took a lecture from my godfather, Bobby, to show me the power of index funds rather than some class. That is not to say you cannot learn it in a course, though.

Thought

People will think differently of me for investing in index funds.

Response

All you have to do is show them Warren Buffet's words on index funds. Besides, the opinion of others regarding your financial portfolio doesn't matter all that much.

Thought

What is Zack getting out of this?

Response

I am trying to make the average investor more educated. Someone did it for me, and I want to pay it forward. Specifically, I want my brother to become a better investor. He has not yet taken my advice, and I think the best way to convince him is to write a book. I am not earning a commission from some firm; the only benefit I receive will be this book's proceeds.

Thought

My dad said our advisor has made him a lot of money, and he can take care of everything.

Response

I repeat again: All advisors are not created equal. There are some decent advisors out there who are legally obligated to put your best interests first. If you need them for the emotional part of staying in the market, they may be a wise choice and can help you in the long run. Always remember they come at a cost, and a good one will be hard to find. I will not cover the differences in financial advisors, but if you are adamant about needing one, Tony Robbins's book *Unshakeable* offers an excellent section on the topic.

Thought

These numbers do not make sense. This will never work for me like Zack is saying.

Response

Look up the return statistics for yourself. Run the numbers in a compound calculator yourself. I tried to present the numbers in a simple and powerful format to help you understand where each number is coming from and why. There is no guarantee associated with investing, but I find the historical trends to be very compelling.

Thought

The market is down right now.

Response

Good news! That is the best time to invest! You are buying low. It does not matter when you invest, as long as you have compounding and time on your side.

Thought

Who is this Zack person? He did not get his PhD at Harvard. I have never heard of him.

Response

Warren Buffet. You know him, right? If you do not want to follow my advice, follow his. I am only giving you the user's guide. Most people do not invest because they do not physically know how or what to invest in. I have shown you physically how to navigate a website, given you words of emotional encouragement, and showed you the truth through statistics.

If you are still with me, I applaud you for getting this far in the book and learning this much about the topic. Investing is a long-term project; do not fall victim to get-rich-quick schemes or advice. Take advantage of this knowledge. Take advantage of compounding. Take advantage of this opportunity. I believe in you.

Rational Steps

The best thing you can do is follow these steps:

1. Determine an allocation.
2. Regularly invest.
3. Do not look at how much gain or loss you have incurred if you obsess over it, even for "fun."
4. Rebalance when necessary (discussed in chapter 12).
5. Do not listen to "experts" or neighbors when they claim the financial sky is falling.
6. Stay invested, and if you can't, then read this book again.
7. At no point should you ever pull money out of an account unless you are in financial hardship, you want to start cashing in on the account you have built, or to rebalance. I cannot stress this enough.

If you did not do it, mark this chapter now. I mean it; you will need to come back at some point.

Frustrated?

Annoyed?

Bored?

In over your head?

The fact of the matter is this book is about passive investing and why it can produce superior returns compared to active investing in the long run. If you feel frustrated, annoyed, severely confused, or even just bored, then maybe passive investing is not for you.

I want to be an unbiased source because I was once in your shoes, but finding a financial advisor might just be the right thing for you if all of this is too much. You have made it this far in the book, so you understand the ramifications, but I applaud you for taking charge of your financial life.

Remember, indecision is still a decision. I applaud anyone that can take advantage of any of the knowledge I have written thus far. Just remember that the worst place you could be in is with all your savings in a bank, or worse, under your mattress, eroding your purchasing power by close to 2 to 3% a year.

Chapter 17
July 29

Core Principle:
Coming to fruition.

As you all know, I've written this book to help guide my brother towards investing in index funds and getting him away from the traditional advisor route. As of writing this, he has not read this book yet, but I will make sure he will be the first one to have a copy in his hands. I had to polish and finish this book faster than I had planned because of what happened on July 29.

On July 29, I got a call from my dad. He said he was taking a ride to see "David," my family's financial advisor. He wanted to let me know he would not be home for dinner, and I was on my own. Of course, that meant I was going to get Chipotle for dinner. I proceeded to ask my dad why he was headed there, and he said he had Adam in the car. He told me Adam was ready to start investing with the help of our financial advisor.

I quickly ended the call. I thought long and hard about why I had failed to get my brother to take my advice. Then it struck me: All these years, I had never spoken his language. So, Bobby and I devised a different draft of this book to help speak Adam's language, to make the book accessible and understandable to everyone.

At the beginning of this book, we talked a lot about the DiSC test. I hope in the end I have made this book readable to not only the Cs and Ds but also the Is and Ss. As a teacher, I know not everyone learns the same. When a concept seems as clear as day to me, it could be as if I am speaking another language to some of my students. I think this idea of teaching in terms of others' ways of learning has made me a better author and a better teacher. My brother may not have this book in his hands until many months past that phone conversation with my dad, but I hope this book speaks his and many others' language and finally hits home.

I am passionate about changing the financial life of my brother. We have grown up in very different directions, and he has taught me so much without even knowing it. He is one of the most caring and selfless individuals. Honestly, he reminds me of my dad, but unlike my dad, Adam is exceptionally creative. Adam has excellent potential to go very far in more different directions than I ever could. He has taught me so much about happiness and creativity. I love my brother Adam, and I want to finally give back some life lessons.

The world is full of Ds that sometimes impose their methodology on people to get 9-to-5 jobs and not use their creativity. So, to all those Is and Ss, be creative, be spontaneous, and take risks with your passions and imagination. My brother changed my life. I have wanted to write a book for FOUR years now, and he finally inspired me to write it. I believe that if I could just change his life in return, I could change millions more like him (that's you!). I think I have more to offer to my brother than just financial advice, so I will finish this book where my next one starts. Enjoy.

Chapter 18

Beyond Investing

We have now reached the last chapter of this book. In reality, I have told you nothing original. This information is out there in a multitude of different fashions. I have read many books on the topic and done some extensive research. But I believe I have brought all the benefits of those books and research together in the previous pages, making this an informational user's guide to average investors. I have read some great books on the topics, but I felt there was important information and angles missing from each of those books. You now have a complete, straightforward, and robust user guide to implement index investing. I will finish this book in a peculiar way by returning to the concept of compounding. Now, I hope to add an original and esoteric idea that I practice myself. Let us return to an example I previously mentioned.

If you invest $1 a month for 40 years at a return of 10%, compounded monthly, you could expect to earn $6,376.78. And you only invested a total of $480. You only invest $12 a year. Your end portfolio value is close to 13.5 times the amount you put into the account. Let us call this example consistent and efficient investing.

Let's now say you are inconsistent and "sometimes forgot" and invest $1 a month for only six months out of the year, for 40 years at a return of 10%, compounded monthly. So, you only invest $6 a year. You would earn $3,189.39. Not too bad still, but that is also half the value of consistent and efficient investing. Put simply, for the price of $240, you lost around $3,000. Let us call this example inconsistent and efficient investing.

Let us now say you invest $1 a month consistently for 40 years, but you only average 3% compounded monthly. You would earn $931.69, less than one-sixth of the value of consistent and efficient investing's expected value. Let us call this example consistent and inefficient investing.

The best part of indexing is the market. Over the long run, it will yield efficiency. All you have to do is consistently contribute to your accounts. That lesson is all well and dandy, but this chapter is not about investing. This chapter is about the cold, hard value of compounding in your everyday activities. If you cannot wrap your head around compounding with numbers, this chapter may be a little tough to wrap your head around. Let us look at one more example with the numbers, and then I will stray from the example.

Let us suppose you invest $1 a day for 40 years at a return of 10%. For example's sake, let us compound these numbers every single day. Your ending value in the account would be $195,577.67! For a measly $1 a day! The average American household makes $60,000 before taxes. Investing $1 a day is .6% of your yearly salary. Not 6%, but **.6%** of your salary. Less than 1% of your total compensation.

Let me get back on track to my main point, but I hope you will think about it in terms of the numerical examples we have just discussed. I have a belief that being "consistently efficient" in your personal life will yield you outcomes far greater than the initial effort exerted. What do I mean by being consistently efficient? Let us consider someone shooting 500 shots every day in basketball in hopes of joining the NBA. He could just be consistent and devote the time needed every day to successfully shoot those shots.

However, a great basketball player also must be concerned with shooting percentage. If this person just shoots and never counts any of his shots and takes no care to do his best and improve while shooting those baskets, he will most likely never make the NBA—no matter how many shots he takes.

On the other hand, this person is exceptionally efficient and aims to take only well-purposed shots. That is great, but maybe he is inconsistent, and instead of shooting every day, he only shoots twice a week. Perhaps he takes some weeks off. Again, he will most likely never play in the NBA. The third option is that he shoots well-purposed shots and shoots 500 of them every single day. I cannot guarantee he will make the NBA, but if he does this for 10+ years, he is giving himself a hell of a chance.

Why do you care? You are not trying to play in the NBA. My point is this: If you can devote consistency and efficiency to an area of your life for multiple years, you will get farther than you ever thought you could and will put the power of compounding to work to reach dreams and aspirations you never thought you could.

Why do I think the power of compounding works for investing and the effort costs people exert? Because you have already experienced it. How many times in your life have you worked at something for hours, days, or years, and then all of a sudden, things became more apparent, or your progress doubled more in a few days than in the first 30? Compounding is slow to start. After some time, that growth can be exponential. The early few hours, days, or months of anything could be slow, but they will eventually pick up speed and grow faster than you have ever seen before. Just look at the graph below, which illustrates the penny example. Progress will always be slow when you first start anything new. And that's OK.

Nevertheless, you must stay at it. Ask about any successful persons' story: There was a time when they really did not know if their business, career, or dream would work out. Successful companies like Apple, Amazon, and Tesla do not just spring out of the ground successfully. They were built on top of the many failures and setbacks before they got to where they are today. As the old proverb says, anything worth doing will not be easy, and anything easy will not be worth doing.

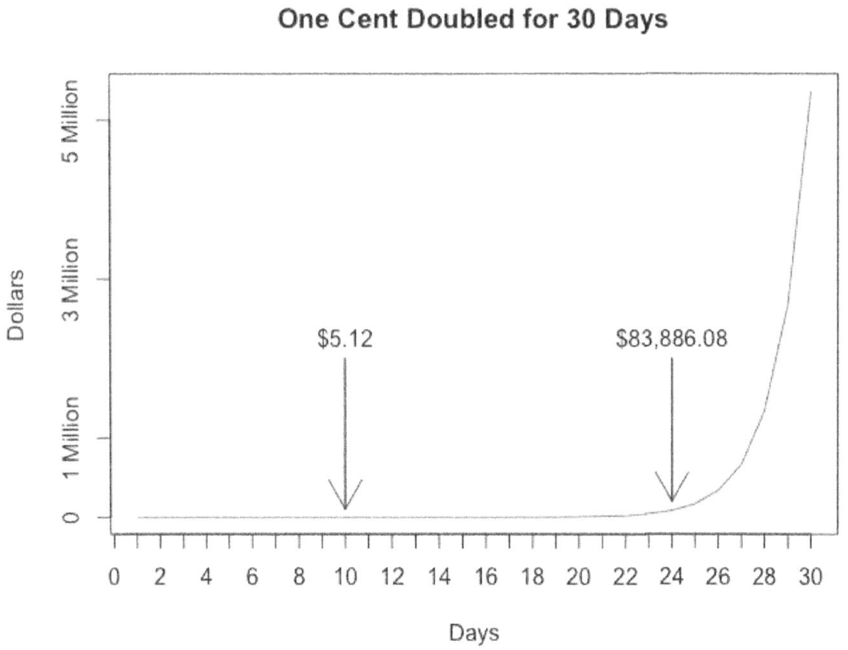

Look at the doubled penny graph. For the first 10 days of the process, one-third of the time, it does not even break $10. For the early 20 days of the process, two-thirds of the time, it does not even break $100,000. However, by the end of the 30 days, there are more than $5 million. In the first third of your process, you may not even break a page into your book. However, you must remember that the foundation of compounding is being built. If you keep at it consistently and efficiently, you will reap the benefits.

The $1 a day yielding $195,577.67 was a metaphor for the way we spend our time each day. Small, measly amounts of time each day can have powerful impacts. If you cannot find an hour to do something, then find half an hour. If you cannot find that, then find 15 minutes. Everyone can find 15 minutes, even if it means turning that show off a little early before you go to bed or waking up 15 minutes earlier. If you find 15 minutes a day, that adds up to over 91 hours of free time a year. That is over 456 hours in five years.

Suppose I told you that you had the next 91 hours to devote to yourself uninterrupted and with the power of compounding. Suppose I said to you that you would yield five times, 10 times, or even 100 times the effort you put in. What do you think you could accomplish? What about over five years?

What I am trying to get you to understand is that your dreams will take work, energy, and effort. If I told you you had 456 hours of uninterrupted free time over the next five years devoted to one mission, you are telling me you could not get that mission accomplished? Our hopes and dreams are incredibly close.

Reach. Step. Achieve.

Thanks for reading.

Appendix

Please note that 25% = .25, 2% = .02, or 97% = .97. When you multiply a number by 1.25, the resulting number will be 25% more than the original number. When you multiply a number by .80, the resulting number will be 20% less than the original number.

Asset	Initial Investment	Portion of Portfolio	Return	Year 1 Amount in the Account	Portion of Portfolio
Stocks	$500	500/800 = 62.50%	49%	500*1.49 = $745	745/1006 = 74.06%
Bonds	$300	300/800 = 37.50%	-13%	300*0.87 = $261	261/1006 = 25.94%
Total	$800	800/800 = 100%		$1,006	1006/1006 = 100%

We now see that our allocation is off by more than 10 to 15% for both our bond and stock portions of our allocation. We can handle this in two ways. First, we could sell off some of our stocks and buy more bonds.

Asset	Year 1 Amount in the Account	Portion of Portfolio	Buy and Sell	The New Portion in the Account
Stocks	500*1.49 = $745	745/1,006 = 74.06%	X/1,006 = .6250 X = 628.74 Sell 745-628.74 = $116.26 of the stocks	528.74/1,006 = 62.50%
Bonds	300*0.87 = $261	261/1,006 = 25.94%	Buy $116.26 worth of bonds	(261+116.26)/1,006 = 37.50%
Total	$1,006	1,006/1,006 = 100%	$1,006	1,006/1,006 = 100%

The second way to handle this is to only buy the asset that is dipping in percentage.

Asset	Year 1 Amount in the Account	Portion of Portfolio	Buy and Sell	The New Portion in the Account
Stocks	500*1.49 = $745	745/1,006 = 74.06%	Do nothing	745/1,192 = 62.50%
Bonds	300*0.87 = $261	261/1,006 = 25.94%	(261 + X)/ (1006 + X) = .3750 X = 186 Buy $186 worth of bonds	(261+186)/1,192 = 37.50%
Total	$1,006	1,006/1,006 = 100%	745 + 261 + 186 = $1,192	1,192/1,192 = 100%

Zack Dorobiala

Made in United States
North Haven, CT
04 November 2026

21732951R00065